# POSITIVE

# PARENTING

The Essential Guide to The Most
Important Years of Your Child's Life

WRITTEN BY
Susan Garcia

# CONTENTS

# Introduction

Parents have for a long time tried to figure out the relationship between them and their kids. While there are many techniques that one can use to strengthen this relationship, positive parenting is the number one way to raise happy, disciplined children. Parents are the most concern with their kids' happiness, but they want to be happy as well.

We want to enjoy being parents and not have such a hard time correcting our kids' behavior. For us, it would be bliss if our kids would not throw tantrums, talk back, did their homework on time, went to bed on time, and collected their toys leaving the house, and their rooms clean at all times. However, this is hardly ever the case, even with older children who know what they ought to do.

We scold, we talk, we repeat, and we give up. Sometimes we decide that sanity is better than all the yelling and policing we are subjected to. "If a day would go by without me yelling, that would be like winning the lottery," we laugh with our friends over coffee.

However, maybe we have this all wrong. Maybe the yelling and talking and nagging are producing more problems than it is helping us raise healthy, disciplined and happy kids. Maybe we need to try another approach.

Imagine starting a kitchen garden to grow vegetables for your family. When you start with your seedlings, it will not look like much. You work your way out to watering, weeding and keeping insects, diseases, and birds away. After a few short weeks, your garden looks beautiful, and your family can enjoy it.

Similarly, raising children is like maintaining a garden. When your child first arrives, they are a blank canvass, like a seed, and how you take care of them by nurturing them through the difficult emotions of childhood determines how they will turn out as adults. Rearing children requires developing effective parenting skills, just like gardening.

Parents have agreed that there is no child-rearing manual, and while this is correct, research by psychologists and social scientists have revolutionized how children are raised by conducting experiments that help us understand children better. Research by Jean Piaget revealed that children do not understand situations in the same way adults do. Expecting children to act like 'mini-adults' and behave will, therefore, get us nowhere.

Is all lost then? Are we stuck with kids who cannot listen and behave the way they should? Is parenting going to be an impossible uphill task? Lucky for us, the answer is no! Children are born ready to learn, and the first person they learn from is you and me. As a parent, modeling good and acceptable behavior is the first step in raising kids. We have heard people say that 'kids will do as you do, not as you say' and it is true. Imagine then what we are modeling when we scold them guns blazing and send them to their rooms amid abuse and threats! Is this how we would like them to behave? So why do we model it?

If we are honest, we have used how we were raised as a foundation for raising our kids. If we were punished, we are prone to punish as well. If our parents were kind and respectful, we are likely to be kind and respectful. While we may carry hurt feelings in us from our childhood, healing these past pain helps us become better parents than our parents. Without healing, we are likely to inflict the same pain in our kids, create the same resentment we feel, and undoubtedly continue the cycle. However, we have to adopt a different method, so this cycle ends with us. By rewriting our past, we can write the future.

Once our past pain is healed, we must rewire our brains to positive parenting. A mental diet is not an easy diet. Like joining the gym, you are going against your body's current and forcing it to start swimming uphill. Charles Duhigg has demonstrated this in his book "*The Power of Habit; Why We Do What We do in Life and Business*." A parent prone to use punishment uses it with so much ease because it has already become a habit, formed slowly from how they were raised to how they have been using it on other kids, their peers, and now their kids.

To break the cycle, and ultimately use positive parenting techniques, we must make a conscious decision to break the habit. Easier said than done, but it is possible. When your child misbehaves, the routine is to use some form of punishment (yell, time-out, threaten, spank). What we want to achieve is connecting with our child, understanding where they are coming from and using the misbehavior as a platform to correct bad behavior and teach a life skill such as anger management, empathy, responsibility, timekeeping, among others.

Emotions are the center of living. Helping your child understand their emotions is helping them live a happy and successful life. We do what we do because of how it makes us feel. Let us strive to teach our kids, every day, how to handle their emotions, and they will learn how to handle their behavior. Before we discipline, we must consciously ask ourselves why did my child react like that? What can I teach? How can I best teach this lesson?

A child does not wake up and decide to be naughty. They have a reason behind every behavior, and they have desires they want to express, just like you and me. By knowing where they are coming from, we understand the desire they wish to be met, and use this as a teaching platform to show kids how to meet their desire without misbehaving.

The journey is only tough when you start. Positive parenting is not something you might be used to and snapping every once in a while, is ok. Like our kids, we are learning a new skill, and every skill takes time to master. The more you exercise a muscle, the stronger it becomes, and a mental muscle is no different. The more we continue to follow positive parenting principles, the more it is engraved in our minds that this is the new default setting.

Positive parenting is not about immediate gratification and instant pleasure, for our kids or us. It's about setting it upright for kids, and ourselves, to enjoy long-term happiness in life. Sometimes instant gratification is what we need, and it is achievable without using punishment. If you are in a public place and your child throws a tantrum, you want them to stop. This is a short-term goal for every discipline act. You also want to make sure that they do not repeat the behavior in question, which is a long-term goal for disciplining your child.

When we understand how our kids' brains are developing, we are better placed to understand that their behavior is either being controlled by their rational mind or their irrational mind. When the irrational mind, also called the reptilian brain, is engaged, your child will not cooperate no matter how much you try. Sure, threatening them and spanking them will get them to stop, but the little fellow is left confused and wonders if being himself is a crime that he must be punished for it. It is everyone's nature to use our reptilian brain, and naturally, we want to either fight or flee. However, that does not mean that we should.

Parents must learn to disengage their kid's irrational mind and engage their rational mind. When emotions are high, let them calm down. Connect with your child and comfort them. Allow them to feel their emotions and then teach them how to handle it better next time. Do not lecture them, instead engage them in a dialogue where you can both look for a suitable solution. You demonstrate patience, mastery of your own emotions, and problem-solving skills, all necessary for a happy child and an equally happy parent.

In every home setting, ideas are bound to clash. Parents are two people from different backgrounds with different beliefs coming together to raise this little human. When ideas clash, it is time to team up and draw a roadmap to guide you in the future. Remember we are not perfect, and we will make mistakes. However, undermining your partner in the presence of your child is confusing the child and losing your authority as a parent. A united front creates stability for the children.

Keeping it together is not always easy. A good parent can often snap and lose it. Everyone has a limit so if you can catch up with a friend, sleep early, take up cycling, jog, go for a swim, and have a spa treatment it will do you good. Live a little away from parenthood. These are great ways to maintain equilibrium. Joining a positive parenting support group would be better if you feel completely overwhelmed no matter what you do. Having someone to exchange ideas with and be honest about your feelings is important. If you need a support group, reach out.

Knowing what to do and not doing it is the danger of learning. It is one thing to pick up a book such as this one and another thing to implement the principals outlined in the chapters to follow. Being a parent does not have to be so hard. It can be enjoyable if you take a step at a time towards raising children in a positive environment that is conducive for you and them. So, don't bite more than you can chew. Start with one thing at a time and keep adding to the list. Parenting is not a sprint; it is a marathon. If you keep training and using positive parenting methods, you will win the race and raise independent, centered children.

# Chapter 1: Discipline vs. Punishment

Children are capable of thinking. The only difference between how their brains work and ours is the level of maturity and development. The guidance of a parent/guardian is a crucial role in helping children develop, especially where discipline is concerned.

Parents sometimes feel at a loss when it comes to getting their kids to act respectfully. Kids often argue, are disrespectful and will climb on the top of the table during dinner whenever they get a chance. As a parent, you often feel frustrated and find yourself uttering the same phrases over and over again. "Don't do that. Stop It! You are going to hurt yourself."

The constant battles witnessed during homework, bedtime and mealtimes is evidence of the struggle parents are engaged in continuously with their children. If you experience any of these frustrations, you are not alone.

Discipline is a fundamental aspect of raising children, but most parents often mistake it with punishment. Discipline comes from the word 'disciple,' which means, to teach, train, or to instruct. Thus, it is an act of teaching children how they should behave and respond to situations emotionally and intellectually.

Parents are encouraged to use positive discipline methods that involve listening, responding and connecting with a child as opposed to reacting to their bad behavior. However, this is not easy especially when a child is not cooperating in a situation where one is tired and stressed up; it is always easier to punish in such cases.

According to the dictionary, punishment is the infliction of retribution for a committed offense. In simple terms, to punish is to inflict suffering as a penalty for bad behavior purposely. That does not sound so appealing, not to you or your child.

Let's take an example; your six-year-old child is out in the yard playing with dirt. She just learned how to plant a seed and nurture a plant, and she is trying to grow cabbage from a random seed she collected yesterday on her way home from school. She rushes into the house all muddy and pulls you to see her plant.

As she was busy with her experiment, you were busy finishing the hours of kitchen cleaning you have been postponing for the last three weeks. Now, it's all muddy and so are your clothes, you immediately react by yelling at her over the mess she has made. "You won't play with mud again if you can't keep it outside" you threaten her as you march her to the bathroom for a scrub.

While this may not seem to be a problem, the damage your child will experience from this punishment is far greater than the benefit of a clean kitchen. Your child is likely to obey you the next time she goes out to play not because she wants to or sees the need to, but because she is afraid of being punished. Psychologically, she learns that power gives you confidence while she should be learning to trust her creativity and have faith in her ability.

To prove that punishment does more harm than good, Ivan Pavlov, a Russian psychologist conducted a social experiment. Every time he fed his dog, he noticed that the dog salivated. In his investigation, Pavlov rang a bell whenever he gave his dog food.

He repeated this many times and then took away the food, and rang the bell on its own. From his study, Pavlov noted that when the bell rang, and the dog received no food, salivation increased.


Charles Duhigg in his book "The Power of Habit: Why We Do What We Do in Life and Business," states that to form habits or behavior patterns you see a cue, follow a routine and get a reward.

In Pavlov's experience, his dog learned to associate the bell (cue) with the food (routine) and satisfaction (reward). This habit, or behavior, is classical conditioning.

If then a dog can associate a bell with food, it is only natural to assume that using a negative consequence and associating it with undesired behavior, will result to the desired behavior due to fear of the negative consequence.

Punishment tends to make children feel bad about themselves and others. Your child concludes that they are treated so harshly because they are bad; they cannot do anything right and deserve what is coming to them. Moreover, since they are not good, it is only natural that they behave in a way that gets them punished.

Duhigg explains that if the cue, routine, reward loop is repeated enough times, the brain goes to an automatic setting and will naturally follow the habit loop when a cue is presented. When a parent uses punishment or discipline to correct a child, a habit loop is formed in the child's brain, in this case, a negative loop.

If you are fond of using punishment and your child never cooperates, the reason could be that the habit has already been engraved in their brain. Your child already knows that the consequence of their bad behavior will be punished and since they already believe (or are starting to feel) that they are bad, a vicious cycle will form.

So, they get into more trouble, and the punishment they receive affirms their behavior, and it becomes their default settings.

Discipline, on the other hand, is the complete opposite of punishment. Parents who use positive discipline work first on controlling their emotions, and respond to their children in a calm, rational way. It takes time to master so don't feel bad if you are not yet there.

For instance, in our previous example, you would have first thought of why your little girl came running to the kitchen and is pulling you towards the yard. She must be over the moon that she has learned to plant a seed and wants to show off. We all want to show off when we do something great.

Instead of scolding her for the mud and mess, the best alternative would be first to see her planted seed. Once her excitement has dropped a notch, you can walk with her to the kitchen and explain why rushing in without considering the hard work you put into cleaning the kitchen is not cool. You will notice that she will nod in understanding as her brain makes all the connection. Do not be surprised if she apologizes and is open to help you clean the mess before she takes a bath.

Using Pavlov's experiment, we can conclude that, naturally, a positive response to an undesired behavior will result in the desired behavior due to understanding and respect.

The difference between punishment and discipline is that, although both methods get the job done, the resulting behavior and mental attitude will differ significantly: the latter will nurture respect and understanding while the former instills fear of consequence.

# Chapter 2: The Main Goals of Discipline

arenting is rewarding when everyone, especially your children, is cooperating. It is valuable, but it can also be stressful. Pre-schoolers and toddlers are curious, ambitious, fearless, and know nothing about safety. This development curiosity is more often the beginning of mischief and misbehavior. Children don't understand the importance of behaving in a certain way.

The goal of positive parenting and discipline is to develop self-control and problem-solving skills for an all-around child. When a child misbehaves, you want them to stop immediately (short term goal) and never repeat the behavior in question (long term goal). It is understandable why most parents use threats and punishment for both short term and long-term discipline goals.

Positive discipline involves making a conscious decision based on pre-determined principles you have thought about and agreed on. With this approach, you meet the short-term discipline goals of clear boundaries and the long-term goal of teaching life skills, without affecting the development of your child in a negative way.

Let's say, for example, your two-year-old, Joyanne throws a temper-tantrum. She wants you to play tea party with her, but you have explained you will join her as soon as you shoot a quick email about something urgent.

She does not understand what is more urgent than a tea party, so she hits you. Most parents will grab the little girl by the hand and sternly warn her that it is not okay to, hit people. Parents may go a step further and give her time-out as a consequence for her misbehavior.

Is this the worst approach? No, it's not. Could it be better!

What you need is a clear roadmap that leads to what you want to achieve when your child misbehaves. Discipline is meant to train. If you dish out rules and give consequences without explanations or considerations, you are achieving very little in teaching behavior but accomplishing much in instilling fear.

The short-term goal of any parent is to get their child to stop misbehaving immediately. In a restaurant setting, you want your child to sit still, order for their meal, eat in peace and have dessert without a fuss. However, with kids, this is unlikely. What do you do when they reach for your friend's cutlery and insist they want your friend's dessert instead? You want your child to stop embarrassing you and eat their dessert using their cutlery. To achieve this, you can either use a threat that will instantly have them stop or use your discipline road map.

By telling your child that you will not go out with them again, you expect that they will weigh the option of being left behind because of misbehavior and immediately fall in line. However, children's rational thoughts are not developed enough to understand this. Your child is likely to feel threatened, hurt, unloved and their choices ignored as opposed to thinking of why they would not want to be left behind during an outing.

A mother once found herself in this situation. While her friend did not mind the little boy using her cutlery or eating her dessert, the mother was determined to use the incident to teach her son how to treat other people and respect boundaries. She politely asked him if he wanted to use a different set of cutleries to which the boy responded yes. She then asked him what he would do if someone snatched his favorite toy car making him think about the other person's feelings and understand that taking other people's things was not okay. He should instead ask politely and request to switch his dessert.

According to Daniel J. Siegel, M.d and Tina Payne Bryson, Ph. D in their book "No Drama Discipline: Whole-Brain Way to Calm the Chaos and Nature Your Child Developing Brain," there are three fundamental questions every positive parent must ask themselves when a child misbehaves.

1. Why did my child act this way?

Using curiosity rather than anger, you can deduce the reason behind your child's misbehavior. Children find it difficult to communicate complex emotions such as anger and frustrations. That is why they will hit you when you can't play tea party when they demand it or throw a tantrum when they can't have a fifth scoop of ice cream.

2. What lesson do I want to teach?

Depending on the situation, you will want to teach your child responsibility, sharing, caring for others, patience and many other lessons. For example, when she hits you because she wants to play tea party, you can use the opportunity to teach tolerance through delayed gratifications.

3. How can I best teach this lesson?

There is no one size fits all for this question. Consider your child's developmental stage, the context of the situation and device a smart way to communicate what you want to teach. Children enjoy role play and using it to teach them life lessons will help them understand quickly and respond positively. When a child is angry or hurt, it is natural that they will not want to apologize immediately they misbehave. Using role-play, you can quickly calm them down and make them more receptive to an apology.

Using these three questions, -why, what and how- you can quickly change your child's behavior in the short term and lay a strong foundation for their decision-making skills for the future. We want our children to make sound decisions in our absence.

Using Duhigg's principle on how habits emerge, positive parenting becomes your autopilot discipline habit. Your child misbehaves (cue) you use your definite discipline roadmap -why what, how- (routine) your child stops misbehaving (rewards).

Misbehave (cue)

Discipline road map (routine)

Good behavior (reward)

Your child uses the same principle to learn skills. He misbehaves (cue) you use your definite discipline roadmap (routine) he learns an essential skill (rewards). With time, indiscipline reduces as your child learns new skills and recalls them whenever he needs to ask you for something.

Misbehave (cue) → Discipline road map (routine) → Essential life skill (reward)

Toddlers and preschoolers forget and sometimes disregard lessons we teach them. At this stage, retaining information is not as easy as with an adult. Even adults do disregard lessons from time to time.

For a habit to form, the aspect of repetition is crucial. Keep repeating the lesson more often, and your child will soon recall it on autopilot. It is tempting to get back to the old blueprint, punishment, especially when you have repeated the lesson so many times. Your child is testing your limits, which is not a bad thing. By showing her that you are not relenting, she will follow your lead and use the lesson you taught. Children do not test us because they are spoilt brats.

When you leave your child with someone else for a few hours, your child is usually well behaved. According to research, this difference is significant because of the level of comfort your child feels when they are around you. While this is not an excuse to misbehave, children test us because they feel safe around us. They are comfortable, and whether they know it or not, it is a perfect learning ground for them. As they move through development stages and you learn to use your discipline roadmap, children become well behaved even in their parent's presence.

# Chapter 3: How it Worked Before

Disciplining children is not a recent controversy. Since time immemorial, parents have been devising ways to keep their children in line. In 1600 through to 1800, parents used what is now called the Puritan discipline method.

Strict corporal punishment was a popular form of discipline, derived from the Old Testament. Proverbs 29:15 "A rod and a reprimand impart wisdom, but a child left undisciplined disgraces its mother" was used as the basis of punishment. Harsh punishment was common in society and homes discouraged children against rebellion to authority. The slightest provocation was enough to whip a child.

Children were expected to be well-behaved, a reflection of their parents. With religion playing a significant role in how children were viewed, parents were under constant pressure to punish their children into acting accordingly. Phrases such as "spare the rod spoil the child" and "a child left to himself bringeth his mother shame" were commonly used to rebuke parents who did not comply with the acceptable mode of punishment.

Puritan children learned that rebellion and challenging their parent was forcing God to condemn them to eternal judgment where they would burn in fire and brimstone. The strict punishment, through physical abuse, would bring them atonement.

Scenes of children being whipped in public and being forced to make public confessions at meetings were common as stated in the research Journal of Children and Family Studies. Children were made to feel guilty for their actions. They were threatened continuously and were believed to have no autonomy. Besides being threatened with the eternal punishment of the soul, children were thought to be born arrogant and needing strict discipline started at an early age to shape them.

Not everyone was pro-punishment. John Locke, an English physician, wrote parenting guides that formed the basis of the positive discipline methods used today. Although his guides were not popular, Locke presented that children resembled a blank table when they were born and were not predisposed to sin.

Throughout the 17th century, Locke encouraged parents to allow children to learn consequences naturally which build self-control and a desire to own their actions through guidance. Locke, who was later named the father of liberalism, strongly opposed harsh punishment with his message.

In the 1900s, child-rearing experts proposed new methods of forcing children into good behavior. A popular way introduced during this time was the scorecard. A scorecard was posted at home and in school with duties and responsibilities a child was to fulfill. "Rising on time, writing to grandma, finishing homework, eating all their food" are everyday duties children are expected to perform. A gold start would be given when the child performed their duties while a black mark would be used when the child failed to do so. Rewards and punishment were then assigned following the scorecard's guidance. Also, children during this time were expected to stand whenever an adult entered a room. During a bus ride, children were to give up their seat and their place in line for a bus. At school, boys got spanking for indiscipline while girls were slapped on the knuckles.

The increase in research and philosophies in child-rearing brought with it its fair share of confusion for parents. Religion still held a fundamental part in their lives, and parents often became confused between following philosophies and their pastors.

Child-rearing philosophies had its shortcomings. They presented conflicting messages on how much permissiveness should be allowed versus how much punishment was to be used. Some theories offered strict rules to form proper eating habits, sleeping patterns, and social tendencies, while others preferred a more gentle means.

Disciplining a child does not require following standards set by status quo. This is the message Dr. Spoke used to encourage parents to trust their instincts in the mid-1950s. By telling parents, "you know more than you think" in his first publication of Baby and Child Care, Spoke advocated for being reasonable, friendly, open and consistent with kids as an epitome for building relationships with other people as opposed to punishment.

Spokes' principle of raising children results in the rebellious teens of the 1960s and 1970s. His beliefs were rebuked by the strict experts who encouraged the authoritarian parenting style. A clear demarcation was drawn between parents who spank and non-spanking parents, a divide that is still evident today. According to research, only 19% of parents in the United States believe in positive discipline.

Looking back at this style of discipline, the punishment adults inflicted on children were unfair and unnecessary. To an elderly who looks back at what life was back then, the society is immoral and disrespectful.

With technology advancement where kids can spend hours playing violent video games, positive discipline is needed now more than ever. To strike the right balance would mean, picking the "good" parts that made children in the 50's so disciplined and combining it with the elimination of negative child influence found today.

# Chapter 4: What is Positive Discipline

You are sited at the dinner table, and you pour gravy on your three-year-old's turkey. As luck would have it, she wanted to pour the gravy herself. Because children are clumsy by nature, you defiantly poured the gravy amidst her request. What follows is a temper tantrum, screaming and throwing hands in the air, pushing the turkey away and crying for what seems like hours. You try your best to calm her down, but she will not have it. Soon, everyone on the table is contributing, some accusing your little girl of spoiling dinner for everyone.

After a long day at work tackling that impossible task, getting held up in traffic for hours and finally managing to cook dinner, you are tempted to shout, "Stop it right now." Are sounds familiar, does it?

Our forefathers had two main responses when faced with danger, fight or flee. Walter Cannon first described this response in the 1920s. Cannon realized a chemical reaction in our body that mobilizes resources within us and helps us deal with threatening situations. Today, this theory is described as a stress response.

A stressful situation such as the probability of losing your job, a group of people running behind you in a dark alley and a looming deadline can trigger this chemical reaction. The fight-or-flight response is a survival mechanism and helps you to either fight or flee for dear life. While this is great for life-threatening situations, the body often overreacts to stressors that are not life-threatening. Work pressure, traffic jams and family challenges are among the most common stressors. No wonder you are not able to keep it together after a long day when your child throws a tantrum!

The natural reaction would be to fight which is exactly what most parents do when they shout "stop it right now." While a discipline challenge can easily make you go into fight-or-flight mode, you do not have to let it take over. This is where positive parenting comes in.

Remember your child is also in fight-or-flight mode. They wanted to pour gravy on the turkey, and now they are angry you did not let them. They are fighting for what they want. Positive parenting is minimizing the child's frustration and reducing undesired behavior. Instead of punishing bad behavior, positive parenting advocates for creatively modeling and teaching children positive behavior. You approach your child with love, empathy, respect, and kindness and use gentle or loving guidance to explain the desired behavior.

Before attempting to discipline your child, take a step back and put yourself in their shoes. When you were three years old, you went through the same uncontrolled emotions. How your parents reacted to your emotional outburst, their parenting and discipline style made you who are today. It is likely that the reaction you are having right now is the same one your parents had. Think about it. How did that make you feel? History always repeats itself. Research has shown that how we parent our children will be influenced by how our parents raised us. Everyone was wounded as a child. Healing these wounds enables us to parent our children as we want.

# Chapter 5: Positive discipline and your child's development

For the longest time, you have told your nine-year-old to make their bed in the morning, but they seem to forget all the time. As you do the occasional rounds to their room to pick laundry, you notice that he made his bed. You smile, pleased that he finally remembered and secretly hope the trend continues. The bed needs a little straightening here and there, but it's straightened nonetheless. There are no toys on the floor, and the room is surprisingly neat. You promise to mention it during dinner and cook him his favorite meal.

After making his bed two days in a row, you walk in to find the occasional mess you were hoping to forget. You sigh and go about your business cleaning, picking up toys and making the bed. Because you have an early morning, your son is still in the kitchen eating breakfast, and you are tempted to march him to his room to clean up before he goes, but should do you do?

Before we answer that, let us take a closer look at children and how they develop.

Raising children is like traveling on an airplane. When trouble occurs, parents are advised to wear their gas masks first and then help their children because children are vulnerable. If you cannot trust children with a gas mask, how about controlling their emotions and actions?

Because of their lack of control, children rely on us to model the way they should behave. Imagine then, the picture we create when we march downstairs guns blazing and march them to their room for not cleaning up. This is not how we would want them to react when someone else did not fulfill their end of the bargain, yet, it is precisely what we are modeling.

When your child forgets to make his bed, you can use the why, what, how model to remind him of his duty without making him feel guilty he forgot to do it. Could he have woken up extremely hungry today and filling his stomach was his priority this morning? Alternatively, maybe his mind was occupied by something else, and he genuinely forgot about the bed.

As you go back to the kitchen to speak with your son, let us consider positive parenting and emotional development in kids.

## Positive Parenting and Emotional development in Kids

When using positive parenting, you share your emotions openly with your child which in turn helps them understand where you are coming from. For instance, during water play at the park, your child may shove another kid and make them cry or rush across a slippery floor carelessly. Instead of embarrassing them in front of other kids, you can talk to your kid about why shoving another child made them cry. However, just before we get to that part, first ask your child why he felt he needed to push the other child. Maybe the other child had a toy he wanted to play with but won't share, making your child jealous and angry. This would explain why your child shoved him and give you a better ground on handling the situation. Jealousy is a complex emotion, and your child may not know how to handle it yet.

In this scenario, the first step would be empathizing with your child's emotions. This helps your child calm down and engage their rational side of the brain, make sense and understand what is happening.

To help them further, name the feeling. Your child is likely to recognize the feeling next time he feels it and may even mention it to you. Also and most importantly, your child will feel a little stronger next time he is handling a strong emotion instead of letting it sweep over him.

"You feel a little angry that he does not want to share, don't you? And a little jealous of him too?"

An effective way of handling emotional situations is to use stories that are relatable to our kids. Anger and jealousy will keep cropping up before your child can control and overcome them. There must have been a similar situation that happened a while back you can use to correct the behavior.

"Well, remember the time your little sister wanted to play with your toy car, and you wanted to play with it too? You did feel a little angry like today didn't you? But allowing her to play with it first gave you a chance to play with it longer right?"

You can use the same principle when your child runs across a slippery floor. Tell them how that made you feel as a parent and explain why it is not good. If an accident had occurred to them, or someone they know, use that story to illustrate the danger and repercussions.

Whether we are aware of it or not, we are continually coaching our children on how to handle emotions. How we interact with our kids helps them process their feelings and those of people around them. Building their emotional intelligence helps our child learn how to:

- Self-sooth
- Have emotional self-awareness and acceptance
- Control their impulses
- Be empathetic

Emotions are a core part of human development, and while many parents find it complicated, it is essential that we embrace this responsibility. Emotions matter and when children can control their emotions, they can control their behavior.

Let's think about our own emotions for a minute. You will not take on a big project at work if you are anxious, you will not start your own business if you are afraid and again you will not solve a conflict with a friend, your spouse or a co-worker if you can't understand their perspective and manage your anger. Your ability to handle your emotions determines the quality of your life, which makes it crucial to teach children how to handle and manage their emotions.

### 0-13 months of emotional development
At 0-13 months, a baby's developmental task is to learn how to trust. They can pick up anxieties (fear)

from you or feel reassured, by your tone of voice, your touch, and movement. When a baby's stress hormones shoot up, from TV, loud noises and angry voices, your loving arms, kind eyes, and secure cuddling will make them feel better and trust that things are ok.

Building trust brings self-soothing, intimate connection and happy moods for kids making it paramount to provide reassurance as regularly as possible. Luckily, your baby's crying drives you crazy, and you are more likely to pick him up and soothe him.

Over the years, parents had been advised that babies learn to self-soothe when you leave them to cry. Scientists, however, claim that just like an adult, constant exposure to stress in babies leads to increased heart rate, reduce oxygen levels and an increase in stress hormones.

Instead of wiring the developing brain of your baby that he is safe, your baby's brain becomes wired for fight-or-flight. When a baby is left to cry, he eventually falls asleep not from self-soothing, but exhaustion. Eventually, he learns that his parents will not respond and asking for help is futile.

A parent who leaves their baby to cry is also likely to find parenting hard. Every time the baby cries and you ignore, you diminish your inbuilt empathy for your baby that enables you to see things from your baby's point of view. This is the first sure step in disconnecting with your baby

It is impossible to soothe your baby every time they are upset, but nature has taken care of this. As you respond and soothe your baby, his body produces a hormone called oxytocin in response to your loving attention. As he releases oxytocin, more oxytocin receptors are produced which help him feel good and calm himself in your absence. This is the hormone responsible for self-soothing, and more it is produced, the easier it is for your child to self-soothe.

So, when your little girl is screaming her head off because she wanted to pour the gravy, the best thing you can do is first sooth her. Take her on your lap and soothe her, allow her to express her disappointment and to feel it. Once her hormones balance and she is calm, explain to her why you preferred to pour the gravy. She will feel loved and safe and understand that your intention was not to hurt her.

This is the same safety and trust she felt when she was young and had no idea gravy existed. Your kind words, loving cuddle, and comfort will reassure her. Everyone will win and have a great dinner.

### 13-36 months Toddlers emotional development

Toddler years are probably the most challenging in human development for both parent and child. If you have been soothing your child when they cry, then you already have a head start in coping with the challenges you will face when your little one is 13-36 months old.

During this development stage, your toddler wants to assert herself and feel that she has an impact on the world and control over her experiences. She is also learning how to love herself, form her own opinions and pronounce them. Your little girl will start to advocate for her desire which many parents are not prepared for.

A curious toddler will often touch anything that arouses her curiosity as they try to figure out what it is and what it does. Many parents find themselves at loggerheads with their kids. Parents see themselves giving warnings and threats more often than they would like to.

 "Don't touch that. Slow down you will hurt yourself. Get down from there. No! Would you be still while I change you? We don't hit people."

And the tantrums will start, from throwing herself on the floor to screaming and more biting and hitting. Parents have been told to ignore tantrums and not reward children when they throw a fit. But the child sees it from a very different perspective. To her, the parents who would rush to comfort her and help when she was stressed as a child have now abandoned her. She has no idea who they are. In all honesty, parents mean well when they do this. They are teaching their children independence and responsibility through discipline. What most parents do not realize is that ignoring their children causes a relationship to disconnect in the relationship they worked so hard to build when their toddlers were babies.

Toddlers can't differentiate between their emotions and behavior and will conclude that they are bad. She interprets that if she does what she wants, she is bad and so, to be loved and accepted she must do what her parents want. This build into repressed shame that can shadow her for the rest of her life.

Toddlers have a lot to deal with in their daily life. They build stress hormones as adults do, but since their intellect is not well developed, they cannot talk it out, work out to release the pressure or rationalize their emotions. So, nature created a way out for them, tantrums. Tantrums help toddlers release emotions and regain equilibrium. Parents make the understandable mistake that tantrums are within their toddlers' control and fail to give their little ones what they need most.

Toddlers don't enjoy tantrums, they would prefer to feel cherished and loved than to throw a fit. Parents have always responded to outbursts using punishment, either threatening the child or ignoring them. While this stops the outburst, it creates deep insecurity in your child that by expressing themselves, you may even abandon them, no wonder they become aggressive, whiny, clingy preschoolers.

Just like toddlers, seating with your child during a tantrum helps them self-soothe and control their emotions. A parent who stays with their child as they tantrum reassures the child that they live in a warm, safe, and loving place. They realize that the universe is friendly and they are accepted.

Through our guidance, children can follow essential rules that will help them get along with others. In the meantime, we must have the patience to deal with their extreme emotional outbursts. We should not allow our toddlers to act upon all their emotions. For instance, being angry and jealous that the other boy is playing with the truck is not a reason to push him. We have to set guidelines on what is acceptable behavior and limit destructive behavior.

### Preschoolers (3-5 years) Emotional Development

You are at a family function with your preschooler. You are happy they are finally in school, and the teacher can help deal with the tantrums they continue to throw every so often. One of your nieces starts to cry and her cousins, including your preschooler, go to comfort him. You hear your little boy shouting to his crying cousin, "Shut up! You are hurting my ears. Alternatively, you are a big girl; you can't keep crying like a baby." Statements he hears you tell him whenever he throws a fit.

This is a common occurrence with children who have learned to suppress their feelings. The baby who was never soothing as an infant reacts easily and throws a tantrum now and then. His parents mean well but are ill-informed and often threaten him with abandonment, so, his radar is always looking out for danger, just in case they make true their threat.

His parents know they will never leave their child, but he does not know that, neither does he have the capacity to process it. He stays on guard twenty-four seven. He is needy and demanding because that is the only way his parents listen to him and not all the time, only when they have had enough of the nagging and tantrums.

He tries to keep his feelings at bay because he has concluded that his parents will not help him with his emotional struggle. But because he is a child and cannot control his emotions very well, he fails miserably at suppressing his feelings which only gets him in trouble because his parents send him for time out to "think about what he has done."

When he sees his cousin crying, he can't take it because his relationship model says that people should suppress their emotions. Thus, he shouts at his cousin to shut up. Some kids wall themselves so much that other people's hurt feelings do not evoke empathy in them.

Preschooler's emotional development stage is learning to be empathetic. When a baby hears another baby cry, he begins to cry as well. Empathy is inbuilt in mammals, we naturally feel what other people are feeling, and we are compelled to help them or look for a way they can receive help.

As the little girl continues to cry, her other cousin pulls her into a warm hug and soothes her, telling her that everything will be okay. When babies receive empathy at a young age, it lays a foundation for them to show compassion to other people. Such a child is comfortable with feelings because she has experienced them at one time or another. The warm embrace from her father reassures her that she will be fine and after she regained her equilibrium, she realizes that it was not so bad, she was fine.

When she sees another child crying, she will naturally handle the situation the way her parents have handled it with her. If she is unable to soothe the crying child, she will call for help. She understands her emotions and can recognize them in other people.

By the time a child starts pre-school, his brain is mature enough to evaluate if a given response is acceptable or not. He still needs comfort from you, but he has learned to self-soothe and use his words to describe how he is feeling instead of throwing a tantrum.

He is likely to wait his turn instead of aggressively pushing other kids so he can go first. He will control himself when he wants a toy another child is playing with and will be the one wiping tears off another child's cheek and trying to cheer them up.

This emotional self-awareness shows that his left-side of the brain (his logical part of the brain) is integrating with his right side of the brain (his emotional side).

### *6-10 years of elementary schoolers emotional development*
By the time a child is six years, their nervous system is almost entirely wired, their logical brain strengthens and can organize and prune thoughts and emotion. They are more organized, can plan and have a steadier self-control mechanism.

According to research, the brain of a six-year-old has the potential to adapt and change. To some extent, it can be retrained. They have built the basic of self-soothing, the ability to trust and empathize. They have already concluded how relationships work, based on their experiences. Elementary schoolers have created strategies to deal with their feelings.

The boy who is not sure if they can trust their parents may be more stable emotionally, but he will occasionally have emotional outbursts easily. They are more fragile than they look and will often replace tantrums with sulking and banging the door behind them as they lock themselves in their room.

Children who have grown up in positive parenting homes can regulate their own emotions and can control them most of the time. They are in charge of their behavior, and their neurology is built to deliver self-soothing chemicals and regulate fear and anger response. They use their full brain power to function, feel comfortable in their skin and with other people's emotions and forming deep human connections easily.

Children encounter many challenges as they develop in a fast-changing world. Elementary schoolers put their emotions to work as they go through these challenges and use it as an opportunity to mature in their emotional intelligence. They pick up cues that cause triggers and store them in their brain to use when a similar situation occurs in the future.

Children with low emotional intelligence have difficulty picking up cues. They have trouble mastering and navigating everyday development task which makes their self-esteem suffer. Unlike their counterparts, children with low emotional intelligence find it challenging to negotiate anger and anxiety and cower from taking on responsibilities.

Because of the maturity that comes with age, children in this development stage do not need their parents as much as they did before which is a sign of relief to parents. They struggle with their emotions internally, but this does not mean that elementary schoolers don't need guidance.

Children at this age easily communicate their feelings and have a full grasp of what is happening to them. It is the best time for parents to help their children master their emotions to full capacity by talking things out and reasoning with their soon to be teens. Parents can teach their children problem-solving skills and reflections by brainstorming on the options available.

Now let's go back to the nine-year-old who forgot to make his bed and often leaves a mess every day.

How do we use positive discipline to change his behavior?

If he has a constant outburst of emotions, it is safe to conclude that his emotional intelligence is still low and he may need a little more love and care than his counterpart with high emotional intelligence. Instead of punishing him or making him feel bad he forgot to clean up his room, a better approach would be to have a conversation about it and look at the options available. If he finds that he gets late whenever he makes his bed and picks up toys in the morning, you can work out strategies to minimize this workload. For instance, sleeping after picking up toys would give him enough time to make his bed in the morning. Also, sleeping half an hour early would mean more rest and a burst of new energy in the morning. He would be more prepared to make his bed and prepare for school.

Is it too late for the child who has grown up with low emotional intelligence? Not! While it is harder to change the brain wiring of an older child, it is possible. It will take patience, love, and guidance, just like a toddler. You will need to validate her action so that she learns how to trust you and to believe in herself.

Let us consider how to help your emotionally sensitive elementary schooler.

It's the weekend. You are helping your elementary schooler with homework; she keeps rubbing her work and changing the topic. She does not want to do her homework, and you can see it written all over her. You give her a pass and allow her to play for a few hours hoping her mind will settle down into doing her homework later on.

By evening, she is complaining that her teacher gave her too much work for the weekend. She complains that the work is challenging and she cannot comprehend it. You look at her book only to notice it is something she has done before. She knows the answers; she doesn't want to do her homework. She tries to keep it together as you have always asked her to but the stress emotions bottling up build too quickly and waterfalls follow.

Because of the use of punishment, you can see her insecurity as she fights to keep it together. She is suppressing her emotions because that is the relationship model she has learned. If you look closely at her, you can see her struggle to keep it together amid the tears, hoping and praying that you do not reprimand and send her to her room.

Generally, children by this age would be able to control their emotions, and that's where the challenge is. An ill-informed parent will punish the child and solidify further the child's insecurities, but as parents learn positive parenting, helping this little girl will take a different route.

The toddler and the preschooler learned to trust by being allowed to feel their emotions. They were taught how to identify and name their feelings and when they were calm, they learned how to handle their feelings through the pep talk their parents gave.

Your elementary schooler has learned to name her emotions though she cannot control them well enough. By getting a meltdown during homework, the best you can do is hug and allow her to calm down just as you would to a smaller child. Once she is calm, talk about why she is finding her homework difficult and ask her to give options for how she would like to handle her homework once you settle on a plan, action it out.

Your preschooler starts learning how to trust you with her emotions. It will take some time for them to open up entirely because she still has her sensor on guard, just in case this is a drill. Give her some time, as trust builds, you will see an enormous change in her behavior and her emotional control.

She will not always need discipline. A single mom was telling me how she had had a rough day at work one day. She was so tired that she slept throughout the morning. Her elementary schooler was up before her and busied herself with toasting bread and attempted to make some tea using the kettle.

Was the kitchen messy? As messy as a child can make it, but breakfast was delicious. Her child was being thoughtful and making breakfast for her tired mom was the best way she knew she would help out. From the stresses of last night, her mom would have decided to scold her for the messy kitchen, completely ignoring her child's kind gesture. What if something blew up and started a fire?

Instead, she validated her child's action by hugging her and thanking her for making breakfast, ignoring the mess in the kitchen. Once they were done with breakfast, her daughter helped her clean up the kitchen, and she told her that making breakfast was great, but she would prefer it if she were present just in case something went wrong and her daughter needed help. At least until she was sure, her daughter could handle simple kitchen appliances without her help.

By validating her daughters' actions and warning her of the danger she unknowingly put herself in, she built her daughters' self-esteem and used the opportunity to teach her responsibilities. As an elementary schooler continues to be validated and helped to handle emotions, she soon builds her emotional intelligence and handles herself and her behavior without feeling overwhelmed.

### *Positive discipline and brain development*

You passed by the store today and picked up two toys for your kids. One gets a red teddy and the other a green teddy. When you get home, you are excited to show your kids their presents. The pair runs down when you walk in excited that you are finally back. You place the shopping on the kitchen table and excitedly exclaim that you have presents for everyone.

"What did you get me?" the girls ask impatiently. You remove the green teddy and hand it to one girl and then the red teddy to the other girl. Suddenly, there is a problem.

"No! It's not fair. No." cries one of your girls. You dumbfounded, and all you can think about is, 'what just happened.'

"What's wrong sweetie?" you ask.

"I wanted the green one. I always get the red one." She cries.

It has been a custom of yours to get the girl's toys in green and red (each their favorite color). It looks like things have changed. What do you do?

To understand how to handle this situation best, let us first understand how the human brain works, more so how a child's brain develops.

When a child is born, they already have a lot of the neurons they will need for the rest of their lives. The brain of a child is 25% the size of an adult brain. Early in their life, children form a lot more synapsis, electrical signals that connect neurons and send messages to and from the brain, than they need. Although not all neurons will make it to adulthood, they allow children to learn things faster than adults do.

Your child naturally fuels the formation of these synapses and decides which one is important and which ones are not by the nurture they receive from you. A synapse strengthens the more it is used. Synapses are made strong through the formation of ideas in the brain and through learning a set of skills.

The things that children often use like walking and language stay ingrained in the child's brain. Because this is the point your child is creating synapses, it is the perfect time to learn skills, including behavior. This is why, how you discipline your child at this stage matters a lot. You want them to keep the skills that will help them throughout their life and prune the ones that will get them into trouble, hurt others and leave them in despair.

The neurologist believes that the brain has three main regions:

The Reptilian brain made up of the limbic area and brain stem. This part of the brain is responsible for your child's bodily function such as breathing, heartbeat, digestion and more complex functions like survival.

The mammalian brain is the emotional brain. It is responsible for strong emotions like anger, frustration, love, rage, fear, anxiety, caring and nurturing. This is what took over when the little girl did not want the red teddy. The reptilian brain and the mammalian brain are also called the lower mind. It is the lower part of the brain that causes your little one to shove another kid when he wants a toy and to hit you when you don't give him the attention he seeks.

The human brain also called the thinking mind, is responsible for learning, reasoning, logic, problem-solving, flexibility, and adaptability, morality, empathy, sophisticated thinking and decision making. This part of the brain helps us live happy, balanced lives and develop meaningful relationships. The very qualities we want to build in our children.

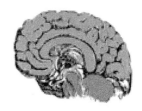

Thinking Brain

Mammalian Brain

Reptilian Brain

These skills require your child to have a well-developed thinking brain, which is where discipline comes in to help guide a child's mind on how to pay attention, think, make decisions, solve problems and also how to interact with others.

The human brain develops fully around age twenty-six. In the meantime, learning and re-learning is the order of the day. As parents, we need to adjust our expectations when it comes to the behavior of our children. If the part of the brain responsible for reliable functioning logic, emotional balance and morality will take twenty-six years to develop, it is only logical to assume that kids will be kids.

They will forget their homework at school, occasionally hit you (or throw a tantrum) to get attention and forget to pick up toys when you have said it a thousand times before. The good thing is, this will not happen all the time. As they practice the skill, their synapses become stronger, and they remember to perform their 'responsibilities' more often.

A developing brain changes every day. To illustrate, let us consider the right temporals parietal junction (TPJ), a part of the thinking brain. When you put yourself in another person's shoes, you engage your TPJ and view the situation from the other person's point of view.

The developing brain of a child will be unable to consider motives and intentions, making it difficult for them to make sound decisions when faced with a problem. For example, the fact that red is the little girl's favorite color and that is why you brought her a red teddy is irrelevant. To her, getting a red toy all the time is unfair.

Our work as parents is to put ourselves in our kid's shoes and see a situation from their perspective before we decide on how to solve the problem. Putting ourselves in their shoes will teach our children to use their TPJ when handling other people.

"You don't like the teddy?" the mother might ask her little girl.

"NO!" she shoots the answer.

If the mother engaged her TPJ, she would know that her daughter does not mean it. She likes the teddy but is not pleased with the color.

At this point, the little girl has already engaged her reptilian brain and is demonstrating strong emotions (frustration, anger, and sadness). Her mother can either escalate the situation or engage the thinking mind of her daughter.

"Well, I'll take it back if you don't want it. You should appreciate that I took the time to buy you the teddy, all you do is complain instead? Give it to your sister; she seems to like toys better than you do, ungrateful little ¬¬......."

Yelling, a form of punishment engages the reptilian brain and only escalates the issue. When the reptilian brain is online, the thinking brain shuts down. In our example, the little girl may throw the teddy on the floor and start a fight with her sister for the red teddy. She may even step on the teddy.

What is fascinating about the brain is that the thinking part of the brain has soothing strands that can calm the reptilian brain when it is reactive. By naming the emotions a child is experiencing, you tame the reptilian brain and engage the thinking mind, soothing the child. Synapses become strong when they are engaged continuously, so by training your child to activate her thinking brain in a stressful situation. You reinforce her synapses preparing her to calm the storm and reflect in harsh conditions.

So, when the little girl melts down over a green teddy, the mother is better equipped if she lets her calm down first by pulling her into an embrace and when there is a deep sigh, you know that the reptilian brain has been sent offline bringing the thinking mind back online. The mother can then take her through the reasons why she chose to give her a red teddy and not a green one. But because the little girl cannot use logic at this time, this approach will probably not bear any fruit, and her daughter will insist that she wants the green teddy.

By remaining calm and empathetic, the mother can explain that her sister will play with her and share the green teddy. On the next trip to the store, she will get a green toy and try mixing up colors, so that they may have toyed with a wide range of colors.

After presenting all this information, the little girl may still be adamant on getting the green teddy, and that's okay. Positive parenting does not always end in roses and rainbows. Our role as parents is to be empathetic and remain calm, once you have explained that she cannot instantly get the green teddy, you can hold her as she completely calms down and joins her sister to play or distract her with something else that will cheer her up.

Positive parenting does not guarantee that you will always get the results you hoped for, what it will do is lower the explosive emotions, reduce the tantrums and avoid any harm that would have resulted from using force and punishment to calm the situation.

The most important thing to remember is that kids are human beings. They have their desires, emotions, and agendas that they are willing to defend. Positive parenting is about being there for our kids and being there with them when they go through a distressing situation. Letting them know that we won't reject or turn our backs on them even when they are at their worst.

Kids, in turn, feel safe and learn to express themselves and develop into independent thinkers able to think through situations, comprehend their emotions and consider other people's perspectives before making a decision.

So, positive parenting helps develop the brain of a child. It strengthens their neurons which makes it easy for them to connect their thinking and reptile brain. These leads to personal insight, responsibility, flexibility, empathy, morality, and sound decision making.

# Chapter 6: The basics of positive discipline

## Connect with your child

Knowing that you are on their side, is what allows your child to risk, learn, grow and be resilient. It is also the secret to being a happy parent. Children do not like commands, but it is impossible not to use commands when we cannot connect with our kids.

To connect with children, parents need to regulate their emotions by healing their wounds. A child's indiscipline does not cause the anger or anxiety that leads to a constant power struggle, fear, and doubt. Our experiences as children do. The tantrum we caused is part of who we are, and they take charge whenever we are upset by the environment we are in.

Our children particularly have a way of triggering these unhappy feelings. We see ourselves in them and the vulnerability we had when we were kids, and we want to do better. But the painful past sometimes overtakes us, and we end up inflicting the same unpleasant experiences on our children. We mean well, but the hard-wiring of our neurons on relationships fail us.

For us, disciplining with love is a foreign concept, and we can't grasp it, at least not yet. By learning to look within and work on our insecurities, we can offer our children the secure foundation that will provide them the foundation necessary to form lasting relationships.

Our deepest fear is to raise unhappy children whom nobody wants to associate with. We fear this so much that we end up being too hard on kids during discipline, to keep them in line and avoid the sharks of loneliness and disappointment. But since we cannot control what happens to our kids, our jobs is to help them build a foundation that allows them to surround themselves with people who will accept them and help them find deep meaning in their lives.

We want to raise children who can control their behavior because they are easy to live with. We wish to rear successful children, not necessarily as society perceives success, but in discovering, honoring and sharing their unique gifts with others. To do this, we must learn to manage our anxieties and give our children the necessary space to discover who they are, build confidence and resilience in themselves.

**Dealing with the past**

To deal with our childhood anxieties and be the parents we want to be for our kids, we need to parent consciously. Pay attention to when kids push our buttons and note it down. Whenever we feel triggered, we stumble on something that needs to be healed. We don't want to repeat the cycle. We want it to end with us so that our kids will have an easier time raising their kids.

To break this cycle, we must learn to pause, take a deep breath and be still. Pausing allows us the necessary time to disengage our reptilian brain and engage our thinking brain. We must pause and think, 'If I react this way, how will I be affecting my child?" without knowing it, we are modeling proper anger management to our kids.

Big emotions are a message that something is not working in our lives. But emotions such as anger do not help us find the best solution to the problem, and that is why anger makes us say and do things we did not mean. The fight-flight mode makes the other person the enemy, and we either want to fight them or flee from them.

When you identify a pain point, you need to reset the meaning of the story. Everyone went through challenging times as children, and it is impossible to go back. What we can re-write is the meaning we took that formed a belief. If your mother left when you were little and never came back, it is time to understand that you had nothing to do with it and nothing you could have done as a child would have brought her back.

The advantage we have now as we look back and reflect at situations that made us angry, anxious or doubt ourselves is that we have grown up. Thus, we have more information now than we did then. We are more rational, and we look at the situation as an adult would. It may take some time to rewrite these painful moments and fully accept the truth we present now, but it is liberating and the only way to not inflict the same pain we experienced on our kids.

Being a parent is hard work and is tougher when you are stressed. Developing a de-stressing system or routine will help us release some of the stress and give us the peace we need to discipline and not punish. After a long day at work, it is easy to take out the stressful meetings we had on our little ones without our knowledge.

Coffee with a friend, cardio workout, meditation, jogging, yoga, or spa treatment will help lower our stress to manageable levels or bring us back to equilibrium. Setting time apart to direct all our aggression on a treadmill instead of our kids may not always be possible. But there are other ways to do it. Put the kids to bed early and have a quiet time where nobody is asking you questions or expecting anything from you, or catch up on some sleep. Blast some music and dance with your kids without a care in the world who will see you. Take a step back and slow down. Sometimes, you don't have to be in a hurry as such.

Sometimes, working through the old is overwhelming, and it may weigh you down. Even as parents we need support and an opportunity to talk about the hard work we are doing, our fears and anxieties and not to be judged for feeling the way we do. There is no shame in needing a support system, reach out, it helps.


### Connecting vs. Spoiling

When parents heal their painful pasts, and they are de-stressed, connecting with children becomes easy. Parents always wonder if all this positive parenting will spoil their kids and they end up with little brats? It is essential to identify what spoiling is and what it is not.

Spoiling has nothing to do with the time, attention and love you give your child. It has nothing to do with respect, independence and right decision making. An infant is not spoilt because you hold them and meet their needs when they cry. Responding to and soothing a child, nurturing your relationship with your child will not spoil them.

Spoiling occurs when a child is raised to feel that they must get their way whether that involves disregarding other people's needs or not. A spoilt child will expect their needs to be met instantly. She will expect everything to be done for her when she needs it and how she wants it. That's not what we are advocating for here. We want our kids to expect that their needs will be met, but we do not want them to assume their desires and whims met all the time. They will get what they need even when children don't understand what they want. Connecting with your child is about giving them what they need, not what they want.

Spoiling occurs when we praise our kids all the time and overindulge them by giving them too much stuff, spend too much money on them, and saying 'yes' all the time. It occurs when we give our children the notion that people will serve their whims.

Parents confuse indulge and connection. When we give children what they want all the time, we deny them the opportunity to learn resilience and deny them the joy of knowing that they have to work for what they want. Things are not just given; you work for them. We deny them an opportunity to learn how to deal with disappointments, yet the world is bound to disappoint them many times over and over again. They become entitled instead of grateful and will be ill-prepared to deal with life when things don't turn out the way they wanted.

When playing in the park, your son throws a fit because he is jealous of a toy another child is playing with. Asking the other child's mother if your son can have the toy so he would calm down is spoiling him. You deny him a chance to learn how to work out his anger and jealousy.

When your little girl cries her heart out in the grocery store for a sweet that gives her tonsils, and you buy it anyway, you are spoiling her. She learns that as long as she throws a tantrum, her needs will be met, even when they put her health at risk.

When you call a parent to ask if your son can get invited to a party he heard about but was not invited to, you are spoiling him and denying him a chance to learn how to deal with disappointment.

Connecting is walking through the hard times with your child and being there for them when they cannot control their emotions or behavior. We are building independence by understanding our child's emotional control struggle and guiding them through it instead of reprimanding them for losing control. When they feel safe and connected, their neurons wire in a way that builds emotional and rational skills to face what life brings their way head-on.

When your child has an outburst and hits her sister because she would not share a toy, hugging her and helping her take a breath to calm down is connecting.

When your son throws his truck towards a jar, hopefully, he missed it, because he is angry and you say "I understand you are upset and having a hard time controlling your anger because you can't take your truck to school" is connecting.

Refusing to give your child ice-cream on a cold morning and allowing her to cry it out as you hold her is connecting.

## How to connect with your child

Parents are human, and with the busy life we live today, it is easier to meet the most basic needs of a child without putting effort to meet emotional needs. To help us connect with them at a deeper level, we need to be deliberate about it. As a parent, you can:

- Have routines that reconnect you with your child during the day like snuggles in the morning or after an afternoon nap.
- Give an emotional refuel before you separate with your child. Hugs and kisses before you leave for work, during bedtime, and before you drop them to school.
- Physical touch such a simple hug. Hug them in the morning when they wake up and in the evening before bed, hug them before you go to work and when you come back just because hugs are awesome and help us connect.
- Do not interact with technology when you have a special time with your child. She will know that she is so important that you put aside your phone to listen to her.
- Have family time almost every day if not every day. Dinner time can be reserved for the family. Stop working before dinner time so that you can play and connect with your kids. Switch off your phones and the television during dinner to avoid distractions so that your family can have your full attention.
- Spare a special time for your child. Spend time with each child individually from time to time. Play a game, go out for ice cream, make your child laugh, or dance and sing.

- Connect to their level and adjust to your child's emotions. It is impossible for children to come up to your level, so go down to their level and connect from their state.
- Do not withdraw, even when your child drives you away. Without nagging or pestering them, let them know you are there for them and you will help them work out their emotions when they are ready.

**Set clear firm limits in a loving and respectful way**

Setting boundaries without hurting our children can be a task. We would rather dish out commands on what they need to do and how they should get it done. It's so much easier.

"Don't hit your sister."

"Fasten your seatbelt."

Sometimes kids feel justified even when they have done something wrong. For parents who are transitioning from spanking to positive parenting, setting limits without punishing your kids when they misbehave, especially hitting other kids poses a challenge.

When they do something wrong, they are spanked; that is the model they know. So, when someone does something they feel is wrong; naturally, they will punish them.

John was playing with his toy once when he suddenly started hitting it. "I said it's time to sleep. I should not repeat myself." This may be the exact words, or something close to what his mother uses when scolding him. John felt the need to spank his toy because it was not cooperating with his bedtime.

Ivy and Nina were playing with dolls when Ivy hit her sister.

"Nina it hurts when you hit someone. Please don't hit your sister" may be answered by "Why can't I hit her, but you get to hit me?".

"I know you feel bad your sister does not want to share. But hitting hurts, that's why I don't do it anymore, and I am sorry I used to hit you. It hurts when you hit someone; please don't hit your sister."

What you have done is that you have admitted your mistake, which made you connect with your child and set the boundary on hitting other people by repeating that they should not beat their sister. A strong-willed child will continue to argue, and it will take you a real effort to remain calm.

This does not mean that you should allow your child to behave the way they want, just because they cannot control themselves, that would be irresponsible. A visit to the toy store is both enjoyable and challenging. Imagine your child throws a tantrum because you won't buy him a toy you feel is too advanced for him.

Telling your child that they seem upset would not help the situation. This will allow him to hold everyone captive, which is not fair for the other parents shopping for toys. It also empowers your child to continue throwing a tantrum, hoping that you will give in to the demand.

"I can see that you are disappointed that you will not be getting that toy. I can help you if you let me. You are now connecting to your child's emotions (disappointment) and offer help, allowing your child to calm himself while reassuring him that you are there for him. Does this mean you get him the toy? No, if the answer was no before the tantrum, it should be no after the outburst.

This way your son learns that there is a limit to what he is allowed to do, touch, engage with and behave like. He also determines that there are no compromises just because he has thrown a tantrum or is disappointed with something. Connecting with kids emotionally makes it possible for us to help them make good choices and respect boundaries.

Children's instincts are not to hold everyone else, hostage, because they feel out of control. We can teach them that relationships flourish with respect, consideration, cooperation, and compromise. Please pay attention to their internal world while holding on to the standards will see children learn connection and respect boundaries.

**Good children and bad behavior**

In the 1950s, children were thought to be inherently evil and harsh punishments were used to correcting their bad behavior. With time, parents realized that there is no bad kid, just bad behavior. This statement is the foundation of positive parenting. Children are learning limits and how they should behave. Their bad behavior is an experiment and an opportunity to determine what is acceptable.

When playing with other kids at the park and your son hits another child, you feel embarrassed and fear that your child may be a mean person. Notice that a child will also feel bad when they hit another child, and they cry. The pain the other child feels is mirrored, and they feel sorry for their actions. Although they do not understand motives well, they already think that maybe hitting the other boy was not a good idea and your child is already regretting it (though he can't accurately pinpoint what they are feeling).

Calling your child, a bad boy or bad girl reinforces the negative feelings and form a negative image of your child in your mind and your child's mind. You might have heard a parent say "my son is very aggressive and hits people a lot; that's just the way he is." This parent has accepted that their son is 'bad' and is likely to reinforce the same feelings in her son.

However, your son may be experiencing a stress trigger that made him act out. Maybe he was angry the other boy took his toy or said something means to him. His environment must have contributed to his outburst causing him to misbehave. Accepting that the behavior was bad, but the child is good, makes positive parenting easier.

Finding out why your son hit another child will make him feel accepted and heard, then tell him the acceptable behavior he should have shown.

"I understand that you felt angry he took your toy. Instead of hitting our friends, we ask them politely to return our toy."

It would be nice if your child replied with "Yes mom, I understand. I promise to use my words next time and restrain myself from harming other kids," but this is not likely. If your child is already feeling guilty about what they did, they are likely to start crying. If they are still angry, they will talk back.

Please do not lose your calm, continue to engage your child's thinking brain until they are entirely calm and understand the lesson. If they cry, hug them to make them feel safe and accepted at their most vulnerable time. Whichever the reaction you get, in your mind and your child's, you have planted a seed that it was bad behavior, not a bad child.

**Give guidance and offer choices**

Children like to feel that they are in control of their lives. They don't want to be given commands all the time. By giving them choices, we empower our kids and show them that we trust them to make decisions.

When going out for a walk, you want your child to be in comfortable shoes and clothes. Asking her to choose which pair of sneakers she wants to wear and whether she prefers to walk in tights or shorts will reduce the hustle. If she picks out what she wants to wear, she will wear it quickly or cooperate as you help her.

A word of caution though. Be sure that you are comfortable with the choices you give. Giving a child an option, you cannot abide with makes you unreliable in their eyes. If you become fond of this, your child will soon start answering you with "I don't know or just choose for me" which shows that they feel that even if they say what they want, you will shoot it down and make your own choice anyway, so why bother?

Parents can start by giving choices that are not too complicated like what shoes to wear. Some decisions like what to cook for dinner may be too complicated for toddlers. The likelihood of choosing a healthy meal is slim, and frankly, they will probably want to eat out than wait for you to cook boring broccoli. A great trick to use is to give them two options to choose from especially when you will be preparing a meal they like. When you do decide to eat out, asking her to pick her lunch or the restaurant to eat at will automatically work.

Adele Feber and Elain Mazlish in their book "How to talk so kids will listen and listen, so kids will talk" stated that giving children choices fosters independence and autonomy. Each decision they make gives them control over their life. Children are entirely dependent on us, but when a person is wholly dependent on another, feelings of helplessness, unworthiness, frustration, anger, and resentment emerge. To reduce a child's bitterness, we should offer them a choice about how something is done.

"I can see you dislike this medicine. Would it be easier to take it with some juice?

Choices give our children the needed practice in decision making. As adults, they will be expected to choose their career, a mate, where to live, their lifestyle and how to tackle problems at their workplace without our help. Through the choices we expose them to, they are likely to feel more confident about themselves and the choices they make in the future.

When you respect your child's choice, he is likely to struggle to see it through and ask for help when he hits a dead end. However, giving an option is not always easy. The sheer convenience of doing everything to save time or get it over and done will tempts parents, all the time.

We live in a busy world that requires us to move at high speeds all the time. It's just easier to wake our kids, choose what to wear and dress them, tell them what to eat and always remind them to hurry up or they will be late.

But protecting our children so much takes away their hopes, dreams, and aspirations and may hinder them from achieving their goals. Choices let them know that they are not entirely helpless, but separate, responsible, competent people.

Another challenge we face as parents are; allowing our children to fail and feel disappointed when we would have told them what to do. We think that their failure is our own and we give in to the temptation of moving in and helping before they ask for our help.

"What should I do?" your elementary schooler asks when she shares a problem she is having with her friends.

"What do you think you should do?" would be an excellent place to start. As they figure out the solution to the problem, sit still and listen. It is tempting to interject when they go with something entirely off but don't.

By asking "how will he feel about that" will remind them to look at the situation from their friends' point of view and consider his feelings. Your daughter will then go back to looking for options.

**Bribes vs. Praise and Encouragement**

As a parent, you will have the most impact on your child's development, both physically and emotionally. Your child's mental health will depend on how you raise them which makes it crucial for you to do your best when he is growing up.

Praising a child is like using a double-edged sword. Praise has some inbuilt problems of its own. It can make you doubt yourself. For example, let us assume your child comes back from school with a drawing. She did not put much effort into drawing it but just scribbled something because she was bored. When going through her book, you notice the picture and say "wow, this is a good drawing Joanna." Remembering what little effort she put in it, Joanna immediately doubts herself, probably thinking that you are either lying, or you don't know what a good drawing looks like.

Praise can also lead to anxiety. Let's assume that your child cannot color coordinate and will put on clothes in the weirdest color combination. Today, however, he walks into the kitchen with a white shirt and blue jeans. You are impressed that he did not pick a red shirt with green pants again. "Good job on the color coordination" you affirm. John sulks and thinks how bad he will feel next time he does not coordinate colors right.

Praise can make your child doubt themselves, can be threatening and make them focus on their weaknesses instead of their strength. It can also come out as manipulative where your child wonders what you want from them. Paul Donahue, Ph.D. says that constant praise poses a risk of putting your child on a pedestal. The child feels pressured to get your approval all the time and continuously look for validation.

When praise is sincere and focused on the effort, not the outcome, giving it as often as possible will not harm your child. The approval is in the effort, not the finished product. When a good habit has already been engraved in your child, you do not need to keep praising him for it, instead, praise him when he does something out of the ordinary, especially where the real effort has been used.

When he gets on a new ride in the amusement park, you can mention in passing how brave he is, but don't overdo it since he is not working hard but having fun. When he practices shooting hoops every day, runs drills and makes a few more baskets today than he did yesterday, praise him, he worked hard for it.

Experts agree that cash should not be used to praise or reward behavior. If we say to our kids "I will give you $5 if you get an A in geometry," we are teaching them to be motivated by money rather than positive feelings on success. Instead, we should use this as an opportunity to celebrate their hard work and achievement. We can take them out for ice cream or special meals after a good game or good report card, which would encourage persistence and hard work.

When giving praise, statements such as 'what a beautiful drawing,' 'good job,' 'that's brilliant' and 'way to go' are neither specific nor evoke the encouragement we want our kids to feel. The more extravagant the praise we offer, the more our kids are likely to reject it as not genuine. People, not just children, perceive words that evaluate (good, beautiful, fantastic, brilliant) as uncomfortable.

According to Adel Feber and Elaine Mazlish, praise comes in two parts. The first part involves using a description with an appreciation for what you see while the second part consists of the child praising himself after hearing the description.

"You cleaned your room? What a good girl you are" becomes "I can see much work has been going on here. All the clothes are in the closet, the blocks are back on the shelves, and every marble has been picked up".

When you describe your enthusiasm, your children learn to appreciate their strengths. It will take a lot more effort to use description when praising than it does to say great or excellent. The more you do it, the easier it becomes second nature.

According to Feber and Mazlish, you can add to the description one or two words that sum up the child's good behavior, telling the child something about himself and the skill he is developing. For instance, your child loves cake, but they only ate one piece.

"You only ate a little slice of cake even though you like it, that takes willpower." Here, your child learns that you appreciate that they did not stuff themselves with cake and they discover that they are developing willpower.

The good boy is quickly taken away by a bad boy, but a thoughtful description of the card he made his mother when she was sick will never be taken away, it is stored in his emotional bank. This memory becomes the go-to emotion when his teacher asks who wants to make a goodbye card for the kid transferring to another school in a different state. It becomes his go-to place when he is faced with a creative project at work when he is an adult.

Because we are teaching children how to behave, parents tend to be quick to point out what a child did wrong and slow to praise. But when you look at the world, it is as swift to offer criticism as we are. Being different at home is the best place for our kids to learn to assert themselves and affirm their rightness.

Self-esteem is built on real accomplishment. It drives from knowing that we have what it takes to share our gifts with the world and make out dreams a reality. Self-esteem is not a one-time feeling. It is an acquired state that comes through repetition and becomes a way of life. It is easy to assume that some children are more goal-oriented, talented and self-motivated than others but this is a result, not a cause.

All children are born with talents and the more they learn how to enjoy the creative process of making things happen, whether they succeed or fail, the more their resilience and self-esteem is built. Some children find it more challenging to learn how to read, remember their backpacks and build relationships. Supporting this child in areas, they need help and praising them when they do well build up their esteem and gives them the confidence they need to keep trying every time they fall.

Sometimes, our parenting skills fail us and the only way to act at the moment is to bribe our way out of the situation. While most parents use this from time to time to get out of a problematic situation, experts advise that we are teaching children to get rewards for behavior they should have.

Laura Markham, Ph.D. says that all of us, including children, need an incentive from time to time to give up something we want. Just because we want our kids to obey us the moment we want them to do something does not mean they will. We are likely to do something when we know there is a reward in it for us, and for our kids, this could be an ice cream treat after leaving the park.

To make this work, Markham says that we need to look for a win-win situation where we reward in advance and not in the middle of misbehavior. Rewarding in the middle of misconduct teaches children to misbehave, so they get a reward.

Parents should, however, use incentives with caution. When children are rewarded for the desired behavior, we communicate that the behavior is unpleasant since you have to be rewarded for doing it. Whether you praise them for doing something they did not want to do or reward them, kids will only cooperate when you are watching, if you use this model of discipline.

Reading can be enjoyable, and a shower is refreshing, broccoli can taste good. Instead of manipulating with a bribe, it is best to use other positive discipline methods like pointing out the result of the behavior. "That is an exciting story. Or "Julie was pleased when you shared your doll with her."

While using incentives is not entirely discouraged, using them as a way out all the time to avoid challenging behavior is not encouraged. Children learn faster than adults do and giving them rewards to good behavior all the time trains them to do what we want so they get something.

When your five-year-old asks you what's in it for her or negotiates with you for a reward, so she does what you want, you have taken the reward too far. Your child still holds all the feelings that are causing her to misbehave inside her. While a reward is a good distraction, be ready to connect with her later and work out the feeling. This means that an incentive can only be used during an 'emergency.' A dinner party at your friend's place may be an emergency, but a store visit is not because she will soon be using tantrums to extort bribes every time you visit the store.

### Teach emotions

Children are born with emotional reactions like crying, hunger, pain, and frustration and learn about key emotions from emotional, social and cultural context. During birth, children have eight primary emotions wired into their brains. These are fear, joy, anger, sadness, surprise, disgust, interest and shame. They express these emotions in different variations such as anxiety which is a form of fear and resentment a form of anger.

Secondary emotions (anxiety and resentment) stem from the eight primary emotions and are used to reflect emotional reactions to specific feelings. A child who is punished because she threw a fit may feel anxious to express her anger or jealousy the next time she gets triggers.

Our reaction to our children's emotions determines their emotional intelligence. As discussed in an earlier chapter, kids will behave better when they learn how to express their emotions. But how exactly can we help them express these emotions?

By giving them a framework that helps explain their emotions. This framework helps kids tame their emotions and use their logical mind to solve problems. It's hard to teach kids about their emotions because emotions are an abstract idea, difficult to explain. Sadness, fear, and excitement are hard to explain unless we use 'emotion teaching aids' to help kids identify them.

Emotions affect every choice a child makes. A child who can understand and identify their emotions finds it less likely to have a meltdown. If they can name it, they can tame it. If your child tells you that he is mad at you, he is less likely to hit you when you do not pay attention to his needs immediately. A child who can say "it hurt my feelings when…" is likely to resolve conflict peacefully.

### Teach empathy

To effectively teach our kids how to handle their emotions and behavior, we must teach them empathy, the foundation of emotions. Daniel Gotham says that compassion is the foundation of positive parenting. Compassion gives you the essential backbone to understanding your child and preventing you from using 'past issues kaleidoscope' to discipline your children. Without empathy, children will not feel loved, no matter how much we love them.

Empathy does not only comprise of viewing situations from the other person's point of view. It is also a physical event controlled by the right side of our brain which also controls intimacy and love.

When our stomach leaps, our skin crawls or our heart skips a beat, the insula (connects the heart, the brain, and the digestive system) sends us a message. We feel it in our bodies. A more accurate definition of empathy is, therefore, feeling from the other person's point of view.

Empathy helps a child feel understood, less alone and the experience teaches her the most profound ways that humans connect. Children learn compassion naturally by experiencing empathy from their caregivers. Being empathetic to your child shows him that his emotions are not dangerous and shameful but universal and manageable.

Empathy does not call for permissiveness; setting limits is crucial. Acknowledge your child's unhappiness about the restrictions but maintain them nonetheless. It is essential to your child that you can tolerate his anger and disappointment towards you.

Empathy helps your child get over his upset feelings, and he can begin thinking about solutions by himself without you solving the problem for him. Listen and acknowledge without jumping in with a solution. Empathy will help you manage your anxiety about the issue and take a step back allowing your child to come up with a solution.

Empathy shows that although you understand his feelings, you don't necessarily endorse them. It is not questioning him and probing, but it is experiencing his situation without forcing him to share his feelings. Empathy is allowing him to feel the situation without invalidating his feeling.

### Name emotions

Preschoolers can learn basic emotions. You can start with happy, sad, mad and scared. Older kids can understand more variants of these primary emotions. Happiness will include love, joy, and peace. Fear will consist of terror, anxiety, nervousness, and worry. Sadness will vary as grief, depression, and loneliness while anger will include frustration, bitterness, rage, and despair.

When your child is sad, asking her "do you feel a little sad that daddy left?" will make her aware of the emotion she is experiencing. To reinforce this, read a good book, and ask her what she thinks the character is feeling when she cries.

You can also comment on other people's emotions, as long as you do it in an accepting and nonjudgmental way at the park when the little girl hurts her knee and cries for her mother.

"That little girl hurt her knee. She must be in pain."

"Is there something special you can do to help her?"

During the day, create opportunities to talk about feelings by sharing your feelings. For example, you can tell him that you feel sad he does not want to play with his little brother or that his little brother is sad he does not want to play with him.

Use charts with different emotions that help your child identify them and name them. You can play a game where you make faces, and she tries to identify the emotions you may be feeling.

Learning and naming feelings is one thing; managing them is another thing altogether. Just because your child is angry does not mean they should hit their big brother, because she is sad does not mean she should take it out on you or other kids.

Whenever you are experiencing big emotions, primarily because of your child's misbehavior, model how they should deal with it, for instance, you can model how to pause and calm yourself when you are angry by taking a deep breath and remaining silent for a few minutes before you correct indiscipline.

When your child is calm, ask them to come up with ideas on how they can handle triggers that would set off their emotions. "You were disappointed that I would not play with you because I was working on a project. You were so disappointed that you became angry and hit me. When you feel angry and disappointed, what should you do?"

Praise your child when they handle themselves well. It takes effort for a child to say "I am mad at you because... or I am sad because...." When they first use their word to express how they are feeling, praise them. "I like how you told daddy you were sad. He had to apologize for not buying you the pair of school shoes." This will encourage your child to use her words more often than to throw a fit.

## Feelings word chart

| | | |
|---|---|---|
| Brave | Cheerful | Confused |
| Curious | Proud | Bored |
| Disappointed | Frustrated | Embarrassed |
| Silly | Excited | Fantastic |
| Uncomfortable | Worried | Friendly |
| Stubborn | Generous | Shy |
| Satisfied | Ignored | Impatient |
| Relieved | Peaceful | Overwhelmed |
| Jealous | Interested | Loving |
| Lonely | Tensed | Angry |
| Calm | Afraid | Sorry |
| Mad | Joyful | Mean |
| Grumpy | Irritable | Alarmed |
| Awful | Bubbly | Calm |
| Tearful | Moody | Thankful |
| Sympathy | Pleased | Weird |
| Violent | Withdrawn | Heartbroken |

| | | |
|---|---|---|
| Desperate | Relaxed | Miserable |
| Comfortable | Glad | Suspicious |
| Uneasy | Hopeful | Left out |
| Discouraged | Ashamed | Understood |
| Appreciated | Surprised | Confident |

## Choose your battles

Toddlers change a lot between 12 and 36 months. There is a massive change in their cognitive and language skills as well as their emotional development. Emotional outbursts and unpredictable behavior are the order of the day. This emotional outburst can take a toll on parents, understandably because being triggered all the time puts us out of balance.

A lot of the things toddlers do is inconveniencing for parents and knowing when to choose a behavior to discipline, and one to ignore is not easy. Parents have been advised to ignore children during a tantrum to prevent them from behaving that same way in the future. However, we have established that tantrums are a result of unmet needs or big emotions that your child cannot control.

Ignoring children during their hour of need, in the name of preventing future tantrums, is taking us back to 1950 when children were thought to be manipulative, cunning, evil and inherently bad.

While children can learn this undesired behavior and know when to push your buttons to get their way, children are intrinsically good, even when they misbehave.

It is interesting how a child's brain development works. It would fascinate parents to know that children don't remember the last time they threw a fit. They don't remember the last time they climbed up they fell that is why they keep climbing up the ladder no matter how many times you ask them not to.

A child who tantrums and misbehaves is innocent, he is just expressing his unfulfilled needs, frustrations and is probably feeling powerless too. The more you connect with your child during this moment, the more you help them name their emotions, the less likely they are to a tantrum every time they are angry, sad or frustrated.

However, do all inconveniences that children cause need discipline? Let us consider some scenarios.

Scenario 1: It's after dinner, you usually read a book together once you finish doing the dishes. Your plastic items are places within your little ones reach. She picks them up, three at a go and head to the sitting room. She comes back for some more and soon; all the plastic cups are gone.

Scenario 2: You are reading a book as your little one is playing with blocks. On top of your book, you notice him laughing trying to get your attention as he pours the blocks from their holding container.

Scenario 3: You are busy making lunch. The house is awfully quiet so your toddler must be up to something, you go round only to find her perusing your magazines.

Scenario 4: You agree to help your child with a crossword puzzle before starting to prepare dinner. When you are done, he insists on doing a second one.

If a child's needs are being fulfilled, but he continues to be annoying and troublesome, the wise thing would be to be firm and ignore them and let them work out their frustration by themselves. In scenario 4, the child's need to connect has been met, but he insists on more special time.

"I know you are disappointed. I can't help you with another crossword puzzle, but I have to start preparing dinner. The option I see is working on another one tomorrow or Sunday. You choose."

By giving your child an option, he knows that you are not ignoring his need to connect, but dinner needs to get started. Walking away teaches him delayed gratification, and he is likely to choose a time that is convenient for both of you.

A parent is not a policeman, acting like one can drain the energy of us and we find ourselves needing recharge more often than we should. Parents need a break and kids will be kids. They will touch things you don't want them to play with to get a little attention.

So, when your toddler plays with your magazines, or rearranges plastic cups, ignoring them would be more appropriate than disciplining them. You can lock the cupboard later and put the magazines where she can't reach them. This principle should only be used when the child is not likely to harm themselves. If she decides to rearrange glass utensils, you need to stop her before she breaks something and hurts herself.

Sometimes, children seek negative attention. Ignoring the misbehavior diminishes the fun of it and reduces the chance of future misconduct. So, if he pours his blocks for the sheer pleasure of it, then tries to get your attention, ignore him.

A parent should never ignore a child's needs, but ignoring purposeful negative behavior (as long as the child will not hurt themselves) can break you from being a policeman.

## Redirect and be consistent

Stay calm, use your words, connect with your child, let them feel their emotions and know you are there for them. Okay! Got it!

When we read a book, attend a seminar or watch an online video on the positive effects our positive discipline habit will have on our kids, we get a lot of 'aha' moments and vow to live by the discoveries we have made until the rubber meets the road, and we lose it. We wonder, how does something that sounds so simple, like stay calm, name emotions, redirect and connect with our kids require such immense willpower and energy?

The truth is, no one can be 100% consistent in disciplining kids 100% of the time. When your three-year-old throws herself to the ground at the supermarket when half the store is watching, we are tempted to use punishment. However, consistency lets children know what to expect and how to make informed decisions. When they notice our inconsistency, they will keep pocking us, hoping to get a favorable outcome.

She cries for a toy today, and you buy it because you don't have the energy to deal with her tantrum, you have enough stress of your own. You will deal with her later.

The next time you go to the store, she throws a fit for a lollipop, you stand your ground and connect with her, she feels disappointed, but she opts for the healthier apple you offer.

When you take her with you for shopping next week, she is likely to throw a tantrum and demand for something else. Not because she cannot ask nicely, but because she is not sure of the outcome. It's like gambling.

You place a bet and pull the lever, then wait for the machine to give you the results. You are not sure if you will get sevens, cherries or lemons, but if you are lucky, you will hit the jackpot. This uncertainty is exactly what kids are experiencing with our inconsistency. When she throws a fit, she may get an outright no and be reprimanded with consequences and threats. There is also a possibility that she will get something even though it's not what they wanted, but if she is lucky, she will hit the jackpot and get precisely what they wanted.

Behavioral psychologists call this 'variable interval reinforcement schedule.' It is the most powerful type of reward system. For gamblers, the size of the reward keeps varying making it challenging to stop gambling. This reward system works the same way with our kids and makes it hard for them to stop playing the slot machine, which in this case is us, parents.

Children are growing beings. As kids become older, our inconsistency is likely to be viewed as a lack of authority. When children get no meaning behind why they should not behave in a certain way, the discipline you are fighting to instill loses meaning. Kids end up being confused and lack the necessary foundation they need to make sound decisions. Today they are here, tomorrow there and back to where they started. It's confusing and creates insecurity.

Parenting is hard work, and there is no refuting that. Coupled with the messy and chaotic world we live in, we are bound to make mistakes from time to time. We will forge things, confuse dates and sometimes we don't have the energy to deal with our kids' behavior. How can we keep it consistent without losing it?

### Choose one behavior at a time

When trying new parenting techniques, choose one behavior to start with. Biting more than you can chew will get you confused, frustrated and worn out. An emotional crush when you cannot keep it together will do no good to your discipline efforts. Choose what you would see as a high priority issue like anger management, bedtime or stealing, and start with that.

The more you practice connecting with your child as you set limits in that area, the easier it becomes in other areas. You will have the advantages of the snowball effect. The more your child learns to control and name their anger, the less likely they are to hit others, call them names and throw a fit.

### *Foster routines*

Keep the same schedule every day, as consistently as possible. Have regular nap times, meal times, fun times and bedtime, so that your child knows what is expected of them. This schedule will reduce the meltdown and make it easier for him to follow the plan.

If you need to change the schedule to include something different, like a birthday party, playdate or mom's visitor, inform him in advance. An alarm prepares him for a slight acceptable change and may avert a meltdown.

After lunch, a mom bathed her daughter and dressed her up in 'nice clothes.' The confused little girl kept asking her mother what was happening, but her mother would not disclose because she wanted to surprise her daughter with an afternoon visit to her grandmothers'.

When she finally learned that they were visiting grandma, the little girl started crying uncontrollably, not because she did not want to see her grandmother but because she felt that her feelings had were disregarded. She was looking forward to spending time with her mother playing games but now she wouldn't.

A big change, like moving to a new city or the birth of a baby, needs to be handled with more care than a simple addition to the afternoon schedule. The dynamic of having a newborn baby taking all her parents' attention is complex for kids to understand as are the dynamics of moving and leaving all her friends behind. Preparing your child for the significant change that is coming her way will take some time.

Inform them a few months before the change to give them enough time to ask questions and gather information on what is about to happen to them. The more questions and information they seek the better. By the time you pack your bags to leave, or her little brother arrives, she will be comfortable and prepared to face the challenge that comes with a significant change.

### Divert and redirect
Diversion offers an advantage when disciplining our kids. Toddlers have a short concentration span that

you can take advantage of and distract them from whatever they are worried about.

Let's take the little one who has a meltdown about going to grandma's place. Her routine dictated that she spends an hour playing with her mother and she feels threatened that this time is being taken away. To calm her down, her mother can distract her by picking one of her favorite board games.

Mom: "Look, Angie, I found your favorite game?" Once her attention is on you, you can continue with "why don't you carry it to grandma's place so we can play it there?  It will be so much fun."

Little girl: "we don't have enough tiles. We are missing some."

Mom: Oh yeah! What do you think we should do?

Little girl: We can buy some at the supermarket

Mom: I am sure we can. Come on let's go.

Diversion is not only for kids. Parents need it as much as kids do. When you are feeling overwhelmed with all the parenting you have done for the day, taking a walk or a long bath will help you settle anxieties and recharge your parenting batteries.

### Redirect

Children do not understand, 'no,' the same way adults do. According to Dr. Jane Nelson, 'no" is an abstract concept that is counterproductive to a child's development needs to explore their world and develop a sense of autonomy and initiative.

Your child may know you do not want him to do something and you will get angry at him if he does it, but he does it anyway because he cannot understand why he shouldn't. His version of knowing something lacks the internal control necessary to stop him.

According to research by Jean Piaget, children do not understand cause and effect making it a challenge for them to understand consequences and ethics. These higher-order thinking may not develop until the child is age 10.

To illustrate, take two same sizes playing dough and ask your toddler if they are the same and if one is bigger or small. When he agrees that they are the same, take one playing dough and smash it with your hands, then put it down again. Ask your toddler if they are the same. He will say they are not and will tell you that the smashed one is smaller.

This experiment illustrates that our interpretation of an event will be very different from our child's analysis of the same event. At the age of one, your child is at the 'I do it' stage where she develops a sense of autonomy vs. doubt and shame. At age two through six, she develops initiative vs. guilt where she explores and experiments.

It must be very confusing then for a child when they get punished for developing. She wonders if she should follow her autonomy and initiative in exploring the world or follow her parent's rules. Just because they are growing does not mean we should let children do whatever they want, which is where supervision, distraction, and redirection comes in.

We must show them what to do instead of telling them what they should not do.

"When you hit your brother because he ignored you, it hurts. Why don't you tap them instead? Here let me show you how it's done."

For toddlers and preschoolers, supervision, kindness, and firmness are essential tools in disciplining. When your toddler wanders off into the kitchen and comes back holding a knife, spanking and reprimanding him will get the immediate effect of putting the knife down. Will spanking stop the toddler from picking up a knife next time he sees one? Probably not.

Kindly and firmly, direct the young one to more acceptable objects, like his toys and continue to do so until the message sinks in.

### *Redirecting ideas for parents*
- Don't lecture

As parents, we often feel the need to lecture our children and point out what they did wrong and explain in detail what needs to happen next time. We might even repeat it a couple of times or ask them to repeat it to make sure the message is home. The last thing anyone wants, including children, is a lecture about their mistake and pop up quiz after the lecture. The parent will often ask their kids "Are you even listening to me?" during these lectures because all the child is hearing is "Good behavior blah blah blah blah." We must address the behavior obviously, but as we do, we keep it short and precise. Even toddlers don't like lectures and to make matters worse they have no brain capacity to internalize everything you are saying.

Once you address the child's behavior, redirect. By moving on immediately, we avoid giving negative emotions too much energy and instead get back on track. If you need to cover an issue extensively, ask questions and listen to the answer. A collaborative discussion will lead to a better understanding of the behavior and the emotions behind the behavior.

- Address emotions

Kids are sometimes unable to distinguish between their emotions and actions. During redirecting, let your child understand that their emotions are normal. There is nothing wrong with feeling so frustrated that you want to destroy something, but saying it's okay to 'feel like it' doesn't mean you should do it. This distinction shows children that it's what they do after their emotions that determine if their behavior is acceptable or not.

"I understand you are angry at your sister, but snatching her doll and throwing it on the ground isn't how we treat each other. Let's talk about other ways to express your anger."

When we undermine our children's feelings, kids begin to doubt their ability to observe and comprehend what's going on within them, which will leave them confused and disconnected to their emotions. We want them to believe that as they learn about right and wrong behavior, their feelings and experiences will be honored, respected and validated. The number of disciplinary actions will continue to reduce.

- Use descriptions

Going back to what Piaget observed, we have established that kids do not see situations from our perspective. The best way to bring them up to our level is to describe what we are seeing, and our kids will get what we are saying.

"Uh! Throwing the blocks makes it hard to build" would make sense to a toddler while "I still see clothes on the floor" would be easily understood by an older child. Such statements open a door for dialogue and learning than an immediate reprimand. "Do we talk to people like that?"

More often than not, all parents need to do is pay attention to the behavior they are seeing. Children already know how to distinguish right from wrong in most situations. By drawing attention to the behavior, they are reminded of the limits you have set and the expected behavior.

"Looks like Anna wants to color the nose" is not fundamentally different from "Let your sister color the nose" but the former offers advantages over the latter. Your child will not be put into a defensive mode which will awaken his reptilian mind, shutting down his thinking mind. It also allows him to exercise his thinking mind and develop an internal compass.

"Anna is feeling left out sitting all by herself" gives her a chance to observe the situation and determine what needs to happen. This shows our child that we are ready to hear an explanation and gain some insight before we draw any conclusions on the matter. We also allow her to defend herself without engaging her reptilian brain or going into the fight-flight mode.

- Get the child involved

Communication in a disciplinary moment has always included the parent lecturing (talking) and the child ignoring (listening). Discipline becomes much more effective when we initiate a dialogue instead of giving a monologue. With dialogue, we do not forego our authority figures in the relationship.

Let's say your daughter is angry at her little brother and she snatched his truck and throws it across the room breaking it. Once you calm the little boy and connect with your daughter you say something like "Liz, I know that you are mad at your brother and that's ok. Everyone gets mad sometimes. However, when you get angry, you need to control the actions. Throwing other people's things only makes them sad and escalates the situation. Next time you need an appropriate way to express your feelings."

While there is nothing wrong with this statement, the approach is offering a monologue where the mother corrects the behavior, and the child receives the information. What if you involve her in a dialogue?

Mom: You were mad at your brother a while back that you threw his track. What was going on? (connect, respect, understand her feelings)

Liz: I was just furious (feels validated, respected and heard)

Mom: Then you threw his track? (brings attention to the behavior.)

Liz: Sorry, I shouldn't have thrown his truck. (remembers the lesson you have taught her)

Mom: There is nothing wrong with getting angry; we sometimes do. How could you handle it next time? (invite problem-solving)

Initiating a discussion about an issue, especially when your kids know you are cutting back will get your kids invested in the conversation to ensure their interests (read: limits you set) are looked into. Although you will be the final decision maker, children learn that their input is valuable, they are respected, and you trust their problem-solving skills. There are times when you do not have room for discussion, times to allow your child to deal with disappointment, but dialogue ends in a win-win solution.

- Use conditional yes

When there is no wiggle room in a discussion, how you say 'no' matters. A straight 'no' is harder to accept than a yes with conditions. A straight no, especially if spoken harshly will immediately connect to the reptilian brain prompting the child to fight, flee, freeze or in extreme cases, faint. A supportive yes, even when it does not permit a behavior, opens the child to receiving and makes learning easier.

To a toddler who enjoyed the zoo so much, you can say "Of course we can stay a little longer in the zoo with the Lions next weekend when daddy drives us a little earlier to the zoo, but right now we have to leave." Your child will not be getting what they want right now, but at least they will come to the zoo earlier next weekend. Here, you are acknowledging the desire and building structure and skill (delayed gratification).

What would an alternative look like? "I know you want to stay because the zoo has all these great animals. Let's buy a teddy lion so you can play with him during the week before we visit the zoo next weekend."

Your child will learn to be proactive and sense the possibility of the future and create future actions in his imagination to meet your needs as a parent. Next time you leave the park, you might hear him say "I am sad we have to go now, but we will come back next weekend."

Here, you teach your child how to tolerate disappointment when things don't go as they would have hoped, but you are assisting them through their frustrations. Conditional yes will work with older children as well. "I have a lot on my plate right now, so yes let us paint a picture tomorrow when I have more time."

Please pay attention to your tone when denying a child something they want. It is crucial you don't appear arrogant, or the effect will be the same as that of an outright no. A conditional yes show your child that you care about their desire, even when they cannot be met immediately.

There are times we must just say no, but more often than not, we can find a way to give a conditional yes than deliberately turn away our kids. The things kids want for themselves are the very things we wish for.

- Be creative

There is nothing like one size fits all when it comes to parenting. Parents need to be flexible enough to pause and think of various responses and their implications to a situation, putting into consideration our parenting style and the child's temperament and development stage.

By exercising flexibility and creativity, we apply our thinking brain and easily conjure empathy, communication and the ability to disconnect our reactivity (reptilian brain). Humor is powerful to use with younger children. By using humor, you can change the dynamic of the interaction by talking in a silly voice or falling comically. Chasing mom to the car makes leaving the park more fun, especially if she screams and crackles in fear. Playfulness can crack a child's high emotions and calm her, so she gains control of herself.

It works with older children as well. Be ready for an eye roll or two or a sly remark here and there. The brain loves novelty and introducing it to something it has not seen before or expected; it will give its full attention. The minds first instinct is to determine if a situation is safe. When you introduce a new element, the mind goes to what is unique, new or different to identify if it's safe or not.

Humour also communicates the absence of threat which opens us up. Creative approaches come in handy when other forms of discipline are not working so well. If your elementary schooler has refused to do her homework on time, it's time to get creative.

Having a secret language or secret sign that only the two of you know about might make the homework more enjoyable. You can use the secret language to signal your child to start homework, and they signal you back when they need help and when they are done.

Creativity takes a lot more energy than we want to invest, and that's understandable. However, the flip side would be to use an unsuitable method that is not working which will wear you down faster and risk you going back to the default setting of punishment. The truth is, we can often avoid a battle or climbing a discipline hill when we become creative.

- Strengthen their mind

The bottom line is teaching children that they do not need to be stuck in negative experiences or be victims of external events or internal emotions. They can use their minds to take charge of how they feel and how they act. Helping children deal effectively with stressful situations increases their confidence in having a say in how they think and perceive the world.

Research indicates that if you provoke kids with the right mental tools that give them a strategy on how to handle experiences (especially delayed gratification), they are likely to manage their emotions, desires, and behavior better. These children also end up being more successful at school, relationship and as adults.

When children are facing difficult situations, we do not want them to deny that experience or try to suppress it. We want them to communicate and describe their inner experiences, what they are seeing and feeling. We also want them to observe what is going on within them and how that impacts them. We want children to learn how to survey themselves and then problem-solve based on awareness. Studying themselves allows them to own what is going on and not be stuck in a negative experience.

# Chapter 7: Parenting styles and discipline

According to the American Psychological Association (APA), parenting practices share three common goals. The first is to ensure children are safe and healthy, the second to prepare children to become productive adults and the third to transmit cultural values.

Being a successful parent is not an easy job, but whether children become healthy, productive, competent adults depend on environmental and biological factors. There are a lot more influences that determine the outcome of a child. The parenting style you use is an integral part of the equation.

The particular parenting style you use may cause disruptive behavior such as attention deficit, hyperactivity disorders, and conduct problems. The parenting style used in psychology today is based on research by Diana Baumrind, a developmental psychologist. In her study, she noted that preschoolers exuded three types of behavior that were influenced by a specific type of parenting. She identified these parenting styles as authoritative, authoritarian and permissive parenting.

Maccoby and Martin expanded this model and used a two-dimensional framework to make further distinctions on Baumrind's permissive parenting style. This led to two different parenting styles, indulgent and neglectful parenting.

The four parenting styles are further grouped into two major categories: demandingness where parents control their child's behavior or demand maturity and responsiveness where parents are accepting and sensitive to their child's behavior and needs.

**Authoritarian parent**

An authoritarian parent has high expectations of their child and attempts to control, shape and evaluate a child's behavior and attitudes to align with set principals. Although wanting your child to fall in line is not entirely a bad thing, an authoritarian parent shows low responsiveness to their child's need and use commands and punishment to achieve discipline.

When a child questions why she cannot use food color to paint her sun yellow, an authoritarian parent will answer with a "because I said so" rather than giving a logical explanation. The child has no choice or opinion in any matter. The little one is expected to follow orders and commands without questioning or complaining failure to which punishment will follow.

This is the main parenting style used by parents in the 1950s. Although their mode of punishment was extreme than it is today, children in the 1950s had no right to speak unless spoken to, were not allowed to share their opinion and had to control their emotions at all times. An authoritarian parent acts as a policeman, always looking for mistakes and ready to send their child to prison (time-out).

An authoritarian parent is also the judge and jury and will convict their child to whichever punishment they see fit. They attempt to control their child's behavior by monitoring their activity in and out of the home. This is the parent who wants to know every detail of where their child is at all times, who they are with and what they are doing.

They decide for their children, giving the child no room to figure out a solution to a problem by themselves. This parent does not consult with their child when making a decision that will affect the child, but they expect the child to accept the decision without complaining. They are rigid, restrictive, and punitive.

The effect this style of parenting and discipline has on children is enormously negative. Children raised in this parenting style learn to depend on their parents and are incapable of making their own decision. As adults, such children make decisions based on what their parents would do, rather than what is right.

Children in authoritarian homes are also timid, anxious and fearful. They have low self-esteem and will rarely volunteer in class or be comfortable handling a task by themselves. They follow instructions not because they understand them, but because they want to avoid punishment.

These children also learn that their emotions are dangerous and work hard to suppress them. They are likely to develop aggressive behavior because of the harsh treatment they received from their parents. They may also misbehave to protest against their parents, even when they know it's a losing battle and the consequences are dire.

The harsh treatment and punishment also cause children to feel unhappy and dissatisfied with their life. These parenting and discipline styles contribute significantly to the increase in depression and delinquency among children.

**Permissive parent**

Baumrind's research states that permissive parents are non-punitive, accepting and affirmative to their kid's behavior and needs. While these are positive aspects of parenting advocated in this book, permissive parents have one major weakness. They do not have set rules or principals that govern their kid's behavior.

They give their children full autonomy and encourage them to do what they want. Children learn to govern themselves from an early age, but without their parent's sound guidance. They are forgiving and use the philosophy of 'kids will be kids' to rear their kids.

They give privileges when their child begs and allows him to get out of time-out if he promises to be good. They are more of a friend to their child than a parent. While they encourage their children to share their problems, they rarely discourage their kids from making bad choices and never give guidance on how to make good choices.

The lack of involvement, consistency, and confidence in their parenting skills make it more difficult to correct their child's behavior and set firm, clear boundaries. These children are likely to be poor in decision making although they seem more mature and responsible than other kids.

Children raised by permissive parents are likely to fall into depression because their parents are too lenient, though they are supportive because they have no one to teach them how to focus and develop good judgment.

Permissive parents show less care for their kids, and they grow up alone without getting attention, develop low self-esteem, poor problem-solving skills, defiant to rules, no self-control, egotistic tendencies and have problems forming relationships and in social interactions.

Kids will prevent others from using toys and throw tantrums when they are defeated. They will even fight physically with other kids to get their way. Their children lack empathy and will laugh at another child when he cries, then feel confused when they see everyone else concern about the hurt child. Their kids may also have health problems because their parents do not limit junk food.

### Neglectful parent
This parent shows low support and low control for their kids. These parents have little knowledge of what their children are doing and will not set firm boundaries and high standards. They set few rules

and give no guidance, nurturing and parental attention to their children's needs.

A neglectful parent is not always intentional in their neglect. Some suffer from mental health issues such as maternal problems from physical abuse and neglect when they were kids, or suffer from substance abuse. Sometimes, they are overwhelmed with issues like bills, work and managing the household that they find it too exhausting to deal with their kids.

Children receive basic needs but will never have their emotional needs met. The parent is undemanding, insensitive and disconnected to her kids.

Kids suffer from low self-esteem and experience low satisfaction in life compared to their peers. They are likely to fall into depression compared to kids raise from authoritative, authoritarian and permissive homes. The kids are sad and confused about what they should do, how they should behave and often feel helpless.

Kids are anti-social and aggressive and will enter into fights more often. According to research, aggression and antisocial behavior in the United States have been attributed to parents neglecting their children. In 2005, a study by the US Department of Health and Human Service concluded that the majority of parents in the United States use this parenting style which is the least desirable parenting style.

Neglectful behavior encourages delinquent behavior such as stealing, school difficulties and may lead to criminal behavior in adulthood. The children are disrespectful, violent and immoral. They, however, have good relationships with friends because they spend most of their time with them. They feel unloved by their parents and are resentful.

### Authoritative parent

This is the most desirable parenting style. Parents who use this model show high responsiveness and set high standards for their children. They set rules and let children experience consequences naturally. When setting rules, parents put into consideration their children's opinions, making them feel heard and included in decision making. This teaches children to trust their problem-solving and decision-making skills.

Parents validate their children's feelings and help them manage their emotions when they lose control. Children are taught how to use tools and strategies to calm themselves and engage their thinking brain when emotions run high. They learn that just because you are experiencing an emotion does not mean you should act on it. When emotions are high, there is no reason and to engage reason, you must tactfully set emotions aside.

Authoritative parents invest a lot of time and energy in rearing their kids. They offer guidance and look for preventive measures to bad behavior in their kids. They are prone to using positive discipline to reinforce good behavior and encourage it to be repeated in the future.

As a result, their children are happy and successful. They're confident and can express their opinion without holding back while putting into consideration the other person's feelings. They are creative in problem-solving and perform better in school. Their parents help them to build social competences that lead to strong bonds with their peers and good relationships.

Children are likely to own their actions and make amends when they error. They are also expected to look for strategies to prevent the misbehavior in future creatively. They have a sense of responsibility and will be first to help another child when they fall into trouble. They are independent and have a high resilience developed from delayed gratification.

### The exception
Sometimes parents do not fit into one category so don't be worried if there are times you are

permissive, neglectful or authoritarian. While authoritative is the most desired parenting style, there have been some exceptions.

For instance, some kids may have authoritative parents but still perform poorly in school if they are still unable to form relationships with other kids. Human beings have a deep desire to connect with others, and when this connection lacks in school, where kids spend more of their time, kids end up being lonely and feel unloved. They may even doubt themselves and question their ability as they try to figure out why 'nobody likes them.'

Some kids, on the other hand, perform best when they have authoritarian parents and peer support. The high expectations their parents set for them academically, coupled with good relationships form a thriving foundation for their academic excellence.

A child's temperament also impacts the parenting style. A sensitive child is perceived more difficult which tempts many parents to be authoritarian, while this is not always the best model; parents may feel like their hand is forced.

### Conflicting parenting styles and their effect on discipline

At some point, parents are not going to agree on how best to parent their kids. Dad may feel that mom is too strict while mom may feel that dad is too lenient. Parenting styles started evolving in each one of us where we were little children. How we were parented, our experiences and the belief and values formed the approach we use when parenting.

Spouses come into parenting with different experiences, and this is often when conflict emerges where belief, values, and experiences differ. These differences not only strain their marriage, but it also confuses the children on the values and beliefs that they should hold.

Just like how children don't like being attacked, parents feel that their spouses attack their parenting style and make them feel like bad parents. While whether to take away too much screen time may not cause much harm, constant squabbles on how children should be disciplined can lead to behavioral issues in children.

Kids have to go through the different parenting styles and find a balance to avoid upsetting mom as they try to please dad. Either way, children feel the inconsistency is too much work, does not offer clear direction and confuses them which makes them unhappy. Some children who show aggression do so because of the weak link created by parenting styles. One parent may rule with a rod of iron while the other is permissive, or worse, parents may undermine each other's style in front of the kids.

The kids find the gap and exploit it to their advantage. While kids feel that it is working to their advantage, disharmony ends up being a disadvantage because boundaries and consistency make kids settle, behave better and are generally happier.

To create an atmosphere where kids thrive and grow, parents need to agree on the parenting style to use. If one parent is at home and the other at work, the parent at home makes the rules, and the other has to support and follow-through. It would undermine a mom's authority when she announces bedtime and dad starts playing with the kids. This creates inconsistency for the kids and makes mom resentful.

### How to harmonize parenting styles and discipline as a team

- Understand your parenting style

From the four parenting styles discussed earlier, understand if you are a permissive, authoritative, authoritarian or neglectful parent and see where your spouse fits. If you can, do this exercise together and help each other see where they fall.

Share your parenting philosophies and belief so that you understand where your spouse comes from. When you understand each other, you are likely to be more flexible and to make compromises for the good of your family and kids.

- Agree to disagree

Creating rules will mean that there will be agreements and disagreements and compromises to make. Agree on the most fundamental rules and handle the ones you disagree on one at a time. Rules such as bedtime, homework and playdate permission can create a balance before you agree on whether children should be given allowances and how much they should get.

Once the fundamentals are out of the way, a framework is created that makes it easy for kids to have balance and be happier. It also minimizes the chances of kids taking advantage and misbehaving. Once the rules have been set, ask for your child's opinion and allow them to contribute. Be democratic.

- Be a team

"Dad, please don't say, can I have another bowl of ice cream?" can lead to the answer "Let's see what mom thinks about it."

When kids are used to discord, they quickly learn which parent is likely to cave in certain situations. By noticing these triggers, involve your partner in the decision and then present it to your child as a united front. If your partner has already made a decision, back them up even when you do not agree with the decision.

Disagreeing with them in front of your child only creates more confusion for your child and causes resentment in the 'losing' parent. You can always ask your spouse about the decision later and discuss how such an issue is to be handled in the future.

- Be flexible

Parents are not perfect, and mistakes are bound to happen every once in a while. Blaming each other or fighting about it will only escalate issues without solving any problem. Find common ground when your parenting styles clash. Use creativity just as you would when your child misbehaves.

**The bottom lines**

When pregnant and a mom to be is asked whether they want a boy or a girl, the mom often answers with 'I don't care. I want a healthy baby'. While she may be hoping for a boy or a girl, inside, parent's first concern for their kids is their health. The moment you hold your baby in your arms for the first time, you have all these dreams for them, perfect score at school, the perfect mate, great career, and dream lifestyle, but amidst all these dreams, the one thing that parents want is happiness for their kids.

Employing the principals taught in this book; we take a step closer to helping our children achieve this happiness for themselves, and impart it on others. Deep down, people are communal, and we want to live in an environment where we are loved and accepted. We set them on a foundation to understand themselves, others and to be understood and accepted. A child raised in a positive parenting environment is likely to be happier, independent, creative, and confident when they are adults.

To truly have happy children, we must BE happy, allow our kids to be unhappy, give our kids more time than stuff, accept them for who they are, set limits, teach them to build relationships, and most importantly, expect effort, not perfection. It is unfair to put so much pressure on a growing child to be perfect. As long as they are taking steps towards becoming centered, we are doing a good job.

Positive parenting is a journey. While it is best if you start when your child is born, it is not too late if you missed that bus. The idea is to catch up, be ready to do the work and follow-through. When kids grow up, they won't remember what we said to them. They will remember how we made them feel, and when they remember what we said, it is because of how it made them feel.

**Reading list**

Faber, Adele, and Elaine Mazlish. *How to Talk So Kids Will Listen & Listen So Kids Will Talk*, CPI Group (UK) Ltd, 2012.

Ginott, Haim. *Between Parent and Child*. New York: Three Rivers Press, 2003.

Kurcinka, Mary Sheedy. *Raising Your Spirited Child*. New York: Harper Perennial, 1992.

Siegel, Bryson Payne. *No-Drama Discipline*. New York, 2014.

Markham Laura. *Peaceful Parent, Happy Kids*. New York: Penguin Group, 2012.

Duhigg Charles. *The Power of Habit*. New York: Random House, 2012.

Conley Dalton. *Parentology*. New York, 2014.

Siegel, Hartzell Mary. *Parenting from the Inside Out*. New York: Penguin Group, 2004.

Chapman, Cambell Ross. *The 5 Love Languages of Children*. Chicago: Northfield Publishing, 2012.

# BONUS

Thank you for purchasing my book. I have a gift for you. A collection of printable worksheets for your little children for FREE.

Scan the code below